ADVANCE PRAISE

"Generosity opens a place within us that brings out a joy and peace in life which comes in no other way. It is the way God made us. David Roseberry's Giving Up *is a clear, concise, and practical guide to opening a generous space within every believer and every church. I dare every believer to practice these words. Our life and our churches would never be the same!"*

—The Most Reverend Dr. Foley Beach
Archbishop and Primate, Anglican Church in North America
Bishop, Anglican Diocese of the South

*"*Giving Up *is a legacy book, in a way. David Roseberry has collected and handed down his considerable wisdom on the subject of stewardship. But there is more to this book than that. David links generosity to both mission and discipleship in compelling ways. He places the value and practice of generosity at the very heart of the church, at the center of the life of a Christian. I am convinced! I am sending a copy of this important book to every ordained leader in my diocese."*

—The Right Reverend Todd Hunter
Bishop, Diocese of Churches for the Sake of Others

"I have known David Roseberry as a friend, coworker, planter, and leader of one of the largest Anglican parishes in the US . . . and I am so happy to commend his writing. His book Giving Up *will not only challenge church leaders and pastors, but point out a positive and generous way forward.* Giving Up *is a fresh call to be the church . . . not to 'seem to be' the church, and that's an issue we all need to get right."*

—Dr. Ed Stetzer,
Billy Graham Distinguished Chair,
Wheaton College

"One of the marks of the ancient church was generosity! The Apostle Paul understood that one of the ways the love of God and neighbor is expressed best is through the generosity of others for the sake of others. David Roseberry's remarkable book is designed for all church leaders that have encountered a serious financial gap in fulfilling its mission. As a seminary professor of practical theology, I will have this book as required reading for all my classes in pastoral ministry."

—Dr. S. Anthony Baron, Director/Associate Professor of Leadership and Pastoral
Ministry, Azusa Pacific Seminary–San Diego
Author, *The Cross and the Towel* and the *The Art of Servant Leadership*

"As the guy who now leads the church that David founded, I see the fruit of this book lived out in front of me every day. I am amazed at the generosity that is alive and thriving in the people of Christ Church Plano, and I know its source: David's relentless commitment to preach the gospel of the Lord's generosity towards us. Read this book. Here is wisdom that will lead to much fruit."

—The Reverend Canon Paul Donison, Rector of Christ Church, Plano

"While many church leaders are hesitant to talk about money, David Roseberry is refreshingly direct about the inextricable link between generosity and true discipleship. Giving Up offers a helpful analysis of the early church's faithful stewardship, a clear rejection of the pervasive and idolatrous Prosperity Gospel, and an array of wise principles and practical ideas for the local church."

—The Right Reverend John Guernsey
Bishop, Diocese of the Mid-Atlantic Anglican Church in North America

"David Roseberry has won respect across Christian leadership circles because he is not afraid to take on the toughest challenges a leader can face—including the ongoing challenge to lead people in generous and wise giving. This book stretched my thinking and gave me proven wisdom I could put to work right away."

—Kevin Miller, Rector
Church of the Savior, Wheaton, IL
and former Executive Vice-President, *Christianity Today*

Giving Up

DAVID ROSEBERRY

GIVING UP

HOW GIVING TO GOD
RENEWS HEARTS, CHANGES MINDS,
AND EMPOWERS MINISTRY

Published by New Vantage Books
In association with the DRS Agency, Franklin, Tennessee
www.drsagency.com

Unless otherwise indicated, Scripture quotations are taken from The Holy Bible,
English Standard Version. ESV5® Permanent Text Edition® (2016).
Copyright © 2001 by Crossway Bibles, a publishing ministry of
Good News Publishers.

Also cited: The Holy Bible, King James Version (public domain);
the Holy Bible, New International Version®, NIV®
Copyright ©1973, 1978, 1984, 2011 by Biblica, Inc.®
Used by permission. All rights reserved worldwide.

Manuscript development by Thom Lemmons, College Station, Texas
Editorial services by Reneé Chavez, Hendersonville, Tennessee
Cover design provided by LeaderWorks
Interior design and typesetting by Volacious Media, Hendersonville, Tennessee

ISBN: 978-0-9905090-6-6
First printing 2017
Printed in the United States of America

For Fran,
with great love.
As loyal as Ruth,
as lovely as Esther,
and as courageous as Deborah.

CONTENTS

ACKNOWLEDGMENTS

It seems silly to write the following when you know that two things are always true of what publishers call the "acknowledgments." First, no one ever reads them. Readers are busy. Most will want to skip over the thank-you part of the book and go right for the meat. Authors should be happy that they might give any attention at all to the introduction, much less a section like this. But second, I would be embarrassed to list the names of all the people who have helped me understand this material—such a list would be nearly endless.

Still, I am going to give it a try.

I give thanks to the Lord for all the goodness and loving-kindness that he has given to me. As a little boy, I used to sit in our church in a small border town in Arizona and hear words that sounded deep and rich but confused me nevertheless. The priest would always say, "All things come of thee, O Lord, and of thine own have we given thee." I had no idea what that meant. I do now, and I agree wholeheartedly. I have had an embarrassment of riches given to me over my life. Whatever I can do to give back in return, I will do. This book is a token of that sincere desire.

I acknowledge the amazing role that Fran has played in my life. She has been both a dedicated champion and an honest critic of everything I have done that has been worth doing. Oftentimes ministers gather around themselves an echo chamber of support. And certainly, she has been supportive. But Fran has been much, much more. She's been as loyal as Ruth and as lovely as Esther . . . and when warranted, as determined as Deborah. Thank you, love.

I want to thank the people who came within the sound of my voice and the influence of my teaching during my tenure as rector of Christ Church in Plano. I could not have asked for a more willing and patient group of believers. They listened to me preach and teach on the subject of generosity for over three decades. They took it all in . . . and then gave. And they gave more and more, even more than they were able. But the best thing about this church is what the great apostle Paul said about the Macedonians: they gave themselves first to the Lord. Well done, Christ Church. Thank you, my dear brothers and sisters in Christ!

Some of the greatest testimonies I ever heard came from friends who gave themselves first to the Lord and then to a life of generosity. They represent only a fraction of the giving testimonies that I could have included. And every one of them is true. Honest to God.

- One man was so moved by the sermon on the widow's mite that he emptied his wallet into the offering plate. And when he realized he was wearing a nice watch, he pulled that off and dropped it in. (I bought that watch back from the church and still have it as an honored emblem of that sacrifice.)

- One man meets me for coffee every year and tells me his financial walk of faith story for that year. It is always a journey of trust and generosity. You will learn more about him in the conclusion to this book.

- One woman explained her philosophy of money to me. She told me about the money she was trying to amass. She lived in the irrational fear that she would never have enough; she had to work and work and work, and therefore, giving anything was hard. I saw recently on Facebook that she had taken early retirement and was volunteering her time to a local nonprofit.

- One man, unknown to me at the time, told me that the Lord had called him to give Fran and me a study tour of the Holy Land. I didn't believe him. I didn't know him! But when the check arrived the next month, I cashed it and booked the trip. That was in 1994. Since then, we have been back to the Holy Land to lead tours for more than five hundred people. One single gesture of kindness and generosity has exploded into massive blessings for hundreds and hundreds of people.

- One woman left a well-paying job in the corporate world and brought her can-do mind-set to a very unformed parish committee. The impact was nearly immediate. Over the years to follow, that woman led through her faith and built an international ministry that supported a dozen missionaries, wide-ranging overseas ministries, local outreach and Christian charities, emergency pantries, and even an entire diocese the size of Peru. Hurricane Katrina met her match in this servant; she mobilized armies of members and volunteers to give their own time and money for relief.

- Recently, I began working with a man who had sold his business for a profit that was enough to make him comfortable the rest of his life. Nevertheless, he was impressed to set aside a large portion of it for need-meeting ministries that honor the Lord Jesus. After giving more than $600,000 for such work, he wanted to give more. He told me that he has been directed by the Lord to give another $1,000,000. He did. His generosity sparked a denominational-wide movement that kick-started nearly eighty different parish ministries across the United States and Canada. (More about this Matthew 25 Ministry later in the book.)

- One man gave a large sum of money for a chapel to honor the Lord. After the gift was given and the chapel was erected, I called him to express my sincere thanks. I asked him how he was feeling knowing that he had given so much. He laughed out a single, shocking word: Broke! Indeed, the market had suddenly changed and his wealth had collapsed between his offer to give and the gift he gave. But he told me it was the greatest thing he had ever done . . . and soon enough, this shrewd businessman had built back his resources.

True stories. Every one of them. And hundreds more could be told. The reality is that those who really live a life of generosity witness things happen in their lives and to their resources that defy explanation. They see that there are things that God does with a generous life that provide opportunities for the gospel to prosper!

I also want to say something about Ben Gill, my good friend of nearly twenty-five years. He has graciously written a wonderful foreword to this book. But his constant encouragement to me and my leadership in this area of generosity is gratefully remembered. In real terms, Ben taught me more about this subject than almost anyone else. But he didn't do it only from an academic or leadership perspective. He and his wife, Holly, modeled it year after year. Thanks, Ben.

I am thankful in deep and personal ways to Jack and Patty Woodmansee for many things. But one thing stands out now. When our children were young and Fran and I would need a break for a few weeks in the summer, we had a dilemma. We could be gone for a three-week period, but we couldn't afford to go anywhere! One day, Jack gave me a piece of plastic after church. It was his Texaco card. "The gas is on us," he said. It still amazes me how a single act of generosity at such a personal and practical level could mean so much. I still get tears in my eyes when I think about it for any length of time. What a great a gift that was for our tired family and their "running on fumes" father.

I also want to thank the board of LeaderWorks: Mike Allen, Rick Pence, and Todd Dexter. These men said yes when I asked them to serve on the startup board for this new nonprofit ministry. They are brothers in Christ and dedicated to the vision of LeaderWorks. And to the early donors (you know who you are) to this ministry, who give boldly, generously, and gladly, thank you! You are investing in a ministry that can make a difference. I love your support.

I also want to acknowledge that what I have learned about generosity I have learned from the people, sermons, readings, books, articles, blogs, conversations, and meetings I have had over decades of ministry. Some of you may read things in this book, things without attribution that you remember saying to me, preaching in your own church, or writing to me. I admit freely that I am a forgetful borrower of wisdom. And I assimilate it so deeply that I think it is mine! Forgive me. Drop me an e-mail and I'll correct my oversight in future editions.

Also, I have great appreciation for my publisher, David Shepherd; my editor, Thom Lemmon; and my colleague and resident English major, Kolby Kerr. Thanks for your insights and ideas about the manuscript. And to those who wrote their endorsement of this book before it was published, we all share a sigh of relief together. It is done.

Thanks to my bishop, Todd, and my archbishop, Foley. And to John, Ed, and Tony. I was most moved by what Paul Donison had to say. He lives in the aftermath of my thirty years at Christ Church . . . and he is living to tell about it.

In publishing a book like this, one wonders about how many copies will be sold. Plenty will be given away, to be sure. But this author does worry about sales. But I am assured that I will sell at least two copies. Someone will stumble across this and purchase it, no doubt. But my mom will buy another, if only as a tribute of support. Thanks, Mom, for all your support.

My children (Jed and Stacy, Taye and Tray, Daniel, and Liz) are precious to me. Much of what I learned about stewardship, trust, and generosity came during the days of their own childhoods, when we had so little . . . but enjoyed our times so much. Thanks for always wanting me to leave a bigger tip. And thankfully, none of these adult children appear anywhere in this book in a "cute kid" story. But my grandchildren do: Haley, Moses, Evan, Milan, and Finley are arrows in their parents' quivers . . . but they are joyful blessings in mine. My children and grandchildren are proof to me that you cannot out-give the Giver.

Soli Deo gloria,

David Roseberry

FOREWORD

A few years before David Roseberry founded Christ Church, I started a stewardship development company called Resource Services, Inc. Our purpose was to help pastors and congregations raise the funds they needed for their ever-expanding mission and growth. Over the years of our company's ministry, with the work of and partnership with tens of thousands of churches, people gave hundreds of millions of dollars to help their churches grow and reach their communities. And by God's grace, I have prayed with thousands of pastors, asking God to help their churches fulfill their vision and mission for the gospel. I have heard some of the finest sermons ever preached on the subject of giving, stewardship, and generosity. But the ironic thing is that while growing up, I knew of only one reason to give to God. The lesson that was hammered into my heart was this: "Give, or God will get you." Maybe I was too young to listen or too distracted to hear, but I can't ever remember knowing about "giving up" to God (Roseberry's apt title to this book) as an act of love, thanksgiving, or joy. One did not give to God out of a sense of worship. We learned to give to God because if you didn't, you would surely pay the price.

Even after seven years of seminary study, that fear-based, guilt-laden belief was still ingrained in me: "Give to God or else . . ." But it no longer seemed right for my adult life. It didn't move me. It didn't bring the joy and peace I read about in the early church in the pages of the New Testament. I was not a "cheerful giver," as encouraged by the apostle Paul (2 Corinthians 9:7). Neither were the members of my small, rural church. Maybe the Delta preachers of my youth had been wrong. Was there a better way to approach God's people about giving?

One year I tried a different approach to our budget fund-raising. In years past this small congregation had been challenged to give to the budget because God, if not the church, needed the money. If they didn't give, bills would go unpaid, missions would be hurt, and—heaven forbid—the pastor might not get paid.

I remember my first experimental sermon as a young pastor in this small church. I said something like this: "Consider this . . . a God who owns the cattle on a thousand hills doesn't need your money. But we, as believers, need to give; our need is a need for worship! Giving out of a heart of gratitude and love will bring more joy to the giver than could ever be bought. Let's stop giving out of fear and give out of love!"

This impact was incredible. We pledged our budget that year, but there was a new joy about it too. There was a lightness of spirit that caused the people to experience giving in a very different way. Giving became something done out of devotion and worship, not duty and fear.

When other ministers heard what had happened in our church, calls began coming in, requesting me to come and teach their people this easy concept. Finally, a few short years later, I left the local ministry and turned to a full-time ministry of stewardship consulting. Now, some thirty-five years later and almost twenty-eight thousand congregations served, I still believe that simple message: God wants us to know a real joy in giving.

But as I say, I came to know thousands of pastors during my working years leading RSI. Only rarely did I find a pastor who understood this important, joy-filled truth about Christian stewardship and was able, at the same time, to communicate it. David Roseberry was one of those few.

He started a new congregation in the North Dallas suburb of Plano, Texas. Christ Church was small enough to meet in a middle school cafeteria. And he was young enough to ask for the help he needed. My wife and I knew about the church start-up from living in the area. And I also knew that Christ Church might one day be a client. But actually, David found me before I ever attended the church. In fact, he was the first pastor I'd spoken to in eleven years who sought me out to ask for help.

I offered to buy him lunch one day . . . and twenty-five years later, I'm still buying his lunch!

Seriously, though, when we met for lunch, I talked about what we were learning at RSI, my stewardship consulting company. "David, we are seeing the financial needs of churches met by people who are learning the joy of generosity and responding to God's call to give. No gimmicks, no pressure, no fear, and no massive guilt. We have found that people who are given the opportunity, without coercion, will be happy and joyful in their giving."

David got it! His eyes lit up, and he saw something of his future in those comments. In fact, his thoughts started running way ahead of me. He had been searching for a new approach to preaching and teaching biblical stewardship. We sat at the table for almost two hours, working on the backs of paper napkins. It was exciting to see this young pastor understand it and then run with it!

One evening a few months later, he gathered his congregation together and talked to them about his dreams and God's plan for their congregation. He had invited me to share a few things about giving and commitment and stewardship and joy. I was only too happy to speak that night. I could sense these people were ready and excited to give. I gave my testimony about giving. Several others publicly shared their own "giving stories." It was a perfect night filled with inspiration, vision, and commitment. As we left that evening, I gave David a hug and said, "You've got a great start at a great church here tonight. Now, don't go blow it."

As I expected, he didn't blow it. In fact, David and his wife, Fran, continued to grow one of the great churches in America. Knowing full well that they would have back-to-back capital-building campaigns for the next fifteen years, my wife and I even joined the church! We gave as the Lord gave to us; we gave joyfully.

If I were a young pastor today, I would want David as my mentor. He understands stewardship and generosity and how to preach and teach in a very disarming but compelling way. Even if I had years of experience in the ministry, I would want him to sit with me and encourage and plan with me.

And I am honored to call David a great personal friend and faithful pastor to my family and me. And as Holly and I came to know his vision for the church more and more, we found joy beyond joy in our personal giving to God at Christ Church.

And I am so happy to see him carry forward the vision of stewardship and generosity that he has developed and demonstrated in his own life and ministry over the years at Christ Church. I pray that the teaching and perspective on stewardship and generosity in this book will bring joy and blessing to many and bring full honor and glory to God.

And as he begins the new ministry of LeaderWorks, I am even more excited that he has started writing on a subject so greatly needed in today's church: generosity.

—Ben Gill,
Owner/President, Resource Services, Inc. (retired)

INTRODUCTION

This is not a book about how to get your church members to donate more money. Neither is it a book boosting weekly contributions. Those things will happen, undoubtedly, as a result of a strong culture of generosity. But those who are looking for ten easy steps to a bigger, better church budget will be disappointed. There aren't ten steps to a stronger church. There aren't five. There is only one step to the kind of church where vision and mission thrive and expand. And you are about to take that step. It may not increase the size of your church's budget or your personal bank account, but it will surely increase the size of the heart of your church!

In fact, put plainly, this book is about the one step we can all take to see our faith, our families, and our churches flourish in a postmodern, unbelieving world. What is the step? It is the title of this book: *Giving Up*. It is about "giving up" to God, about becoming a church filled with people who are teeming with generosity and eager to put their lives and faith forward for the sake of the gospel.

Every pastor and minister shares a common hope that, as Paul wrote, Christ is formed in the hearts, minds, and actions of His people (Galatians 4:19). In other words, our common desire is that the people in our churches would become who they were meant to be: living, loving, walking examples of the Lord Jesus

Christ, people who would be real and genuine in their faith in Christ.

Let me illustrate:

When our family was younger, we considered enrolling our youngest two children in a school in Dallas. This was not a simple decision for us to make: it was expensive; it was far away from our home; my wife would have to commute back and forth with the children every day. We cared about the level of education they would receive, and that would be peerless. But still, what a hassle! On the other hand . . . we kept praying and wondering what to do.

In our final interviews with the headmaster, we sat across the very formal desk from "the gatekeeper," so to speak. We had worked out the finances, the carpools, the uniforms, and the entrance fees. We were committed; it was going to be her decision. She read over the material we had submitted. These papers represented our entire life, family, faith, and philosophy. The silence in the room hung like a shroud, and I started to get a little nervous. Somebody had to say something . . . right?

I looked around to occupy my agitated mind. I noticed the crest of the school and its Latin motto: *Esse Quam Videri*. I decided to pass the time trying to figure out what that Latin motto meant. My mind went to work on its meaning. The English cognates were noticeable. *Esse* looked like the English word *essential* or *essence*. But I knew enough Spanish to know that it referred also to the verb family *to be*. So I figured I was close to the first word: *being*, or *essence*, or something like that. The next word I took on was the last word: *videri*. It was proving tough to figure out. But in the awkward silence of the room, I simply stared at it. Soon, I saw the everyday word *video* emerge. Hmmm . . . clues everywhere. *To be*, then the word *quam*, and then the word *video*.

Quam was pretty common, I knew. I figured it was some kind of conjunction. *And* or *but* or *so*, or a similar word. That was as far as I could go. I still didn't have it.

Essence or video? To be or to video? I could not get its meaning. I liked the word, though: *Videri*. It sounded like an old name for an Oldsmobile: the Oldsmobile Videri. I was close, but nothing made sense.

The headmaster must have felt my pain, because she broke the silence: "That is the school motto." She said it so fluidly. "It means: 'To be, rather than to seem.'"

"Oh, okay. Cool."

Immediately, my mind went into the pits. *Did I just say, "Cool" to the headmaster? Who says, "Cool" to the headmaster of a school like this? Good-bye, school! Not a chance here.* Was I "cool," or just seeming to be cool? How had I just become the epitome of the motto's implicit critique?

She explained it more. "Reverend and Mrs. Roseberry, we live in a world of images and falsehoods and icons. Here, we believe that education is about finding truth in the midst of a very image-oriented, shallow world. And we believe that God has called us to raise children who will learn the truth because they have been taught to seek the truth."

The motto was making sense to me now. *I* wanted to be a student here!

She continued, "We know that many people grow up to be Christians in name only. But we desire our kids to not *seem* to be Christians, but to be as Christ was, as he would be if he lived right now. Our motto means that we try to help the children become who they can really be, not who they might seem to be."

She finally got around to telling us that our children had been admitted to the school. We signed the papers right away and left the office. *Esse quam videri* would be a motto I would hold in my mind and heart for years.

That is the goal of this book. To help churches and believers be who they are in Christ and not just to seem to be. And it begins with generosity.

That One Generous Life

Throughout his earthly ministry, Jesus lived a generous life. He noticed and commended the many generous people who gave sacrificially. He freely used the generous gifts of others who gave to his ministry. He borrowed the freely offered gift of the donkey colt at Passover and, as prophetically imagined, was laid in the borrowed tomb of the generous Joseph of Arimathea. He chastised the money changers in the temple, who were never generous by any means. And he ripped into those whose seeming generosity was in name only, the showboating Pharisees. They gave money to impress the masses but let their own families suffer in penury.

Once you begin to see and notice the generous Spirit of our Lord, you cannot *un*see it. It is everywhere. He gave his time to the unimportant and broken. He gave a new lease on life to the woman caught in adultery. He gave a few words of honesty and encouragement to the Samaritan woman, and she was never the same again. His parables were stories of generous people doing generous things for others. The good Samaritan was generous. The prodigal son's father was generous. The parable of the hirelings lifts up the generosity of the owner. Jesus gave copious amounts of time to others and always went where he was invited. He was perhaps the most productive person we could ever imagine. And yet, he was never in a hurry. The Scriptures never record Jesus running anywhere. In fact, the only time Jesus seemed to be in a hurry was when he deliberately walked ahead of the crowd (Mark 10:32). Why? Because he was approaching Jerusalem in order to give his life!

He showed his generous heart for others in his deep care for the disenfranchised: those who had been cast aside by the socially, politically, and religiously powerful of his day. It is Jesus who took a little boy's picnic lunch and generously expanded it into a feast for thousands. Jesus was the one who cursed the fig tree for its lack of fruit—its failure to generously supply the fruit it should have (Matthew 21).

As we see his supreme act of generosity on the cross, consider the generosity of our Lord. All traditional "seven words from the cross" are examples of Christ's generous nature. He: (1) gave his mother a new family in the home of his best friend; (2) gave forgiveness to his executioners; 3) gave paradise to the thief who repented; (4) was thankful for the small drink of water that he was given; (5) gave up his Spirit to the Father; (6) in great humility, gave the crowd the satisfaction of seeing and hearing his supreme agony; and (7) gave his life as he declared his work finished.

When he walked the earth, Jesus was doing so much more than fulfilling a list of prophecies—though he certainly did that. But he was also displaying and laying the foundation for the fulfillment of God's vision for his people, announced throughout the Old Testament. God always intended that his chosen people would be a generous offering for the rest of the world: a "sign" to the nations (Isaiah 66:19), a living doorway into God's presence. Since his calling of Abraham as recorded in Genesis 12, God's will for his people has been that they would live for others, would invite into the blessing of the Creator those who do not know him. As God said to Abram, so he continues to say to us today: "You have been blessed so that all the nations of the world will be blessed." So, bless them . . . and do not merely seem to bless them. *Esse quam videri.*

Christ's will for his church is nothing less than the fulfillment of that same mission. We are in the world as an offering—a living, breathing invitation.

Nothing could be more crucial for today's church than recovering Christ's radical call to self-sacrifice and generosity. True generosity in the church and from the church is the vision I describe in this short book. No other single effort has more potential to magnify the church's witness in a grasping, hostile, self-centered world than a return to the humble, other-focused giving that typified the church in its earliest days. If the church can recapture Jesus' original vision of his church as a generous, giving people, we can also recapture the hearts of a fallen world.

Rediscover the Center

But to do this, we will need to reconsider our understanding of the central identity of the church. For the last several generations, the church prioritized evangelism and discipleship above almost everything else. These two values have been like twin engines bolted on nearly every church I can think of. As a church pastor for more than thirty-five years and now a mentor to other leaders, I have been accustomed to look for these two emphases as signs of church vitality. Any church consultant is going to ask at least two questions in an initial conversation: How is the church *reaching out* to others? How is the church *reaching in* to develop its members through study and teaching?

Indeed, evangelistic efforts and small group Bible studies have impacted many of us over the years. We were encouraged to share our faith, and we did! People came to trust Christ because of these efforts. We were urged to join in regular Bible study: to read, mark, learn, and inwardly digest the Scripture of the Old and New Testaments. And we did. God's Word began to dwell in us richly. We grew in Christ. We gained maturity in Christ. I thank my God for the incredible blessing it was to pastor a church for more than thirty years that focused on reaching and teaching.

Every church needs to examine its commitment to these twin engines.

But if we look deeper into the biblical command to go out into the world or dive deep in Scripture, we discover a surprise: a central tenet of the faith is generosity. Put more clearly, whatever the origins of the modern church's emphasis on evangelism and discipleship were, the heart for these activities in the New Testament arises from the virtue and value of generosity as seen in the life of Jesus, the teaching of Paul, and the practices of the early church. God so loved the world that he . . . gave (John 3:16). That's the gospel truth, pure and simple. And that simple truth reverberates on nearly every page in the New Testament.

Throughout the New Testament, the idea that comes through over and over again is that the church grew in strength, membership, and impact, because of some overriding feature that we may have lost sight of: not structured programming; not broadcast communications; not "each one reach one" evangelism. By the power of the Holy Spirit, the first Christians seemed to get what it meant to give up; that is, they gave up their time, possessions, resources, and energy in unprecedented acts of generosity. They were generous. They gave. They gave of themselves . . . and they gave to others. The old word for this is *charity* . . . and they had lots of it!

As you will see, when we get down to the details of how the church lived out its newfound faith, we find that it gave and that it called its members to be givers. We will see that the early church is easily characterized by this central activity: the early believers gave generously. It is as surprising as it is impressive: they gave. This, it seems to me, is one of the earliest lifestyle changes that new Christians were asked to make.

Again and again, we read of their acts of selfless service, their giving hearts, and their generosity. The power of the Holy Spirit was the key to the expansion of the early church, to be sure. But I have become persuaded that the early church had something going for it that has been overlooked today: they had an overwhelming commitment to give as God has given to them. Further, I am convinced that their commitment to generosity, more than sermons, evangelistic pushes, or public square confrontations, is what made the early church succeed against all odds. They were givers—even when giving made no sense in the broader culture (and it didn't!). Their generosity and commitment to serve generously created the magnetic field that drew believers by the thousands.

What if today's church and its members could return to that type of open-handedness, the sort of self-surrendering generosity that typified the earliest Christians? What if, in the midst of a culture that glorifies the self, we were known for being "the people who give"? What if we retooled our local congregations so that they added a year-round emphasis on generosity and service? I think we would see that the practices and values of the early church in Acts 2:42 (teaching, worship, prayer, and community) were the outgrowth of a church commitment to giving and generosity (Acts 2:44). What sort of astounding, countercultural, unprecedented message might this send to a world in such great need?

I hope you'll join me on a journey of discovery. In these pages, we will assess our current cultural climate, surveying the conditions that cry out for a countercultural message of generosity. We will see the paradoxical truth that we are strongest when we give up the most. We will look in detail at the foundational generosity at the heart of Jesus' ministry, Paul's missions, and the early church's service. We'll observe the dramatic effects of the church's inexplicable generosity on the observing society. Finally, we'll talk about the broken ways the church has approached giving and what it could look like to establish an ethos of "giving up" in your church.

The charge of this book is simple. Let us resist the cultural narrative of selfishness that we are immersed in. Let's encourage our churches to do evangelism a bit differently: to proclaim that our great salvation is not just a guarantee of an age to come, but also an expression of God's generosity to us. Let's let our Bible studies actually push us to do something generous and surprising in our churches and communities: give up! My hope is that we can take our offerings, our time, and the outward and visible, missional ministry of the church and give it up, so to speak, as an offering to God.

I hope to underscore this basic, simple idea over and over again in the book you have in your hands. Why? Because ultimately, the church's real power, its best chance to effect change in the world, comes with giving up: offering up to God with glad hearts what he has given us. Giving up is the church's "Manhattan Project." Generosity in the hearts of God's people is the church's weapon of mass salvation.

I believe this. I have seen it in the life of Christ Church, Plano, where I served as founding pastor for over three decades. As the church became more and more generous in all that it had been given, those around us started to take note and pay attention to our mission. And as our members opened their hands more and more to the generous life of offering time, passion, and money, I saw that we opened our own hearts more and more. I saw an entire congregation live out the first-

Giving up is the church's "Manhattan Project." Generosity in the hearts of God's people is the church's weapon of mass salvation.

fruits of a biblical version of the true "prosperity gospel," one that turned their giving into a great gain whereby the gospel itself would prosper!

Frankly, I have seen this virtue most profoundly expressed in my wife, Fran. Generosity is one of her most obvious strengths; it is, as we have come to discover in our marriage, her love language. Those who know her realize at least that much about her. But her giving and serving are expressions of her worship, her giving up to God. She loves because God first loved her; she gives because God first gave a Savior to her.

I hope and trust that you, too, will find the inspiration and imagination for a generous life of faith in the chapters to follow.

CHAPTER 1

GIVING IN OR GIVING UP?

———•———

I wonder if anyone was really surprised when, in 2013, the staid and proper *Oxford English Dictionary* chose "selfie" as its Word of the Year. After all, ever since the personal mobile phone—with its built-in camera—became nearly ubiquitous in 2005, we have seen a steadily increasing flood of images filling our screens: close-ups of the owner's face against whatever backdrop or accompanied by whatever other person the subject deems most significant to the moment being captured. Our society—especially its younger members—is increasingly obsessed with documenting the details of daily life. More and more, we feel the need, bordering on compulsion, to share with the world, via the vast and expanding network of social media, our moment-to-moment impressions, with special emphasis on what we think, how we are affected, and what it all means to us.

Now, please do not mistake me for some sort of curmudgeonly, cell-phone Luddite. As anyone who has visited my office can attest, I own a full complement of modern, digital devices. Furthermore, nothing gives me greater joy than when the message app on my iPhone pings with a picture of one of my grandchildren (wait . . . do they all have devices?). Staying in communication with family and friends, even when separated by large stretches of geography, is a blessing my wife and I treasure deeply. I love technology and what it has enabled us to know and do.

But I worry about it, too, because of what technology is causing us to become. For example, social media has allowed us to become unashamedly self-oriented. And we didn't need much encouragement for that! It not only suggests, but seems to demand, that what is most important in any given moment is that moment's effect on me. Our technology, of course, adapts to whatever we most need or prize. And these days, I increasingly observe that technology is being used to facilitate, expand, justify, and glorify the self. As I see it, this phenomenon has given rise to what I refer to as "selfie theology": categorizing and judging religious experience or teaching primarily by how it aids or hinders my individual process of "self-actualization."

Selfie theology: categorizing religious experience by how it aids or hinders my individual process of self-actualization.

Nothing New

This isn't new. In a way, social media has simply drawn our attention to our well-developed tendency to draw attention to ourselves! If social media had existed in the time of Jesus, we can well imagine this revised parable of the Pharisee and the tax collector (Luke 18:9–14):

> A Pharisee went to pray in the temple. He knelt down, took out his phone, and adjusted his robes so he looked perfectly prayerful. He was about to tweet a pic of his

pious self, but then he saw another guy—a tax collector!—bending low to the ground across the sparsely crowded room. The Pharisee sneaked a quick pic of himself with the now prostrate tax collector in the background. Tap, tap, tap on the brightly lit screen, and off to the cloud it went. His tweet hit his few hundred followers moments later: "#Praying here next to a tax collector! #GoodLuck #NoChance #Loser. Thanking God I'm not him! #Blessed #PhariseePride."

Remember the way Jesus summed up the parable? The tax collector, not the Pharisee, went home justified before God. #Oops.

Can you imagine it? I can! A few years ago, I led the Ash Wednesday service at our church in North Dallas. What a beautifully rich, deeply devotional service it was; the sermon touched on the themes of continuous repentance and humility before God. The music was moving; we sang these words: "Forbid it, Lord, that I should boast / save in the cross of Christ my God / All the vain things that charm me most / I sacrifice them to his blood." I had tears in my eyes as we sang. The service culminated with a somber moment when each person came forward to receive the imposition of ashes with these words spoken by our clergy: "Remember that you are dust, and to dust you shall return." And then, toward the end of the evening service, with a room of eight hundred people, we knelt before our just and merciful God to reflect on our lives, sins, shortcomings, and need for salvation. As one voice, we read the words of King David's famous confession to God, Psalm 51. The service was dismissed in appropriate silence, and people left to make their way home. Lent had begun.

I quietly thanked people for coming and, after about thirty minutes of reflection by myself, went home. I pulled into the chilly garage, turned off the car, and, before I came inside to spend the rest of the evening with my wife, I decided to do what any other person would do in that situation: check my Facebook page. The screen lit up, and in a few taps I was looking at the feed coming over my timeline.

I could not believe what I saw. I was tagged in several messages, a few of which read like this: "Had a totally fantastic time at Christ Church for Ash Wednesday. Now, sharing a drink with great friends at [local bar]. Go Lent! Can't wait for Easter, when I can add chocolate back into my diet." And under these words was a selfie of three girls blowing kisses at their audience, each wearing a mock flirtatious expression. Just over the pencil-enhanced eyebrows of these beautiful girls were the still-visible traces of the ash crosses I had placed on their foreheads earlier that evening! Seemingly, all they had left from that sober, worshipful evening was a smudged, fading souvenir. #GoLent!

My point: our technology may be nudging us further toward self-obsession, but as I intimated earlier, *we hardly need nudging*. We are bent that way to begin with. Self-absorption is one of the most common and sad themes in the Bible or in the history of thought, for that matter. We all began our life in the same way. We emerged from the womb, opened our eyes, and discovered an entire world, all around us—with us at its center. As we live our lives, we each try to define, refine, invent, and reinvent a person and persona that will succeed. And when we die, we close our eyes to a world that we imagine will never be the same because we are leaving it.

Poets have picked up on this self-absorption and self-promotion. Alexander Pope, the famous Renaissance poet and master of the heroic couplet, wrote of our fixation with both our fallen and our fortunate humanity. From college days, as I tried to figure out my own life, I stopped to consider the deep well of his own thought. His "Essay on Man" is both brutally honest and honestly brutal. Here are a few lines from his poem,[1] along with my unauthorized paraphrase in italics:

Know then thyself, presume not God to scan;

The proper study of mankind is man.

You won't find answers "out there" in space with God;
look within.

Placed on this isthmus of a middle state,

The earth is the island between heaven and hell.

A being darkly wise, and rudely great. . . .

This is our nature: wise but with a darkness; great, but
also a rude beast!

Created half to rise, and half to fall;

---

[1] Alexander Pope, *An Essay on Man: Moral Essays and Satires*, epistle 2 (London, Paris, New York, and Melbourne: Cassell, 1905), 25–26.

We were made for God but easily capable of great sin.

Great lord of all things, yet a prey to all;

We are ruler over the entire creation but at the same time its vulnerable victim.

Sole judge of truth, in endless error hurled:

We should know better, because we each are a judge of the truth we know.

The glory, jest, and riddle of the world!

We are of two natures: amphibious, in a way. We are made of the mud of the earth (a jest and a joke) but infused by the breath of God (a glorious being). We are the pinnacle of all creation and also the most complex puzzle in all of creation.

The bottom line is this, says Pope: Look at us! We are awesome creation as well as awful creature. We have taken Descartes's famous edict, "I think, therefore I am," and given the last word to Popeye the Sailor Man: "I am what I am; therefore, I am."

In a sense, all the news that we create and generate about us is about The World According to Me. We can create a world with images that is made in our own image, one snap, one tweet, one post at a time. And everything we post is filtered through our favorite subject: me. "Look at me!" our posts say. "I'm riding elephants in Thailand! I'm at a rooftop party in New York! I'm drinking the best local brew on the planet!" The implied question behind all of this is: Don't you wish you were here with me? Or don't you wish you *were* me?

There is an old joke about two actors who sit down for drinks every now and then. One talks incessantly about himself. One day, he realizes the other actor has been silent. He turns to his friend. "Well, that's enough talk about me. Let's talk about you. What do you think of me?"

This inward turn colors how we see the world outside us. As we've been immersed in the Information Age, we have become experts at selecting streams of information that conform to our preferences and beliefs. According to the American Press Institute, a staggering 88 percent of millennials get their news from Facebook.[2] Of course, that doesn't guarantee that the information is inaccurate, but it is far more likely to come to them through voices whose opinions have been preapproved by the user. Before social media, we witnessed the same phenomenon in cable television, with ever-increasing specialization in channels—we need never hear an idea or opinion we disagree with again. This is only made more possible with streaming channels that create *à la carte* viewing experiences. Our world is both created and curated for us, by us, and through our posts.

The Inward Curve

None of this should surprise any student of history or any reader of the Scriptures. It's vital that we understand our situation not merely as a cultural phenomenon, to be studied

---

[2] "How Millennials Use and Control Social Media," American Press Institute, March 16, 2015, https://www.americanpressinstitute.org/publications/reports /survey-research/millennials-social-media/.

abstractly, but instead to see how it affects the heart and soul of every individual. Because as much as we want to view our age as especially significant or especially afflicted, we know, as the writer of Ecclesiastes would tell us, this is not really anything new (1:9). The struggle is between the fleshly self, with its desires and demands, and the higher-minded self, who is capable of lofty heights; the battle is as old as human consciousness.

If you read a few verses of one of the oldest books in the Bible, you will think it is the latest from *People* magazine or perhaps some scrap of paper from a journal stolen out of the Kardashians' daily trash. The writer of Ecclesiastes (called the Preacher) complains that there is something wrong about life. Even though he has had it easy, he feels deep discontent. His final verdict should sober us all: *worldliness can fill our lives and yet leave our lives unfulfilled.*

The King James Version of these verses is hauntingly beautiful and unforgettable: "And whatsoever mine eyes desired I kept not from them, I withheld not my heart from any joy; for my heart rejoiced in all my labour . . . Then I looked on all the works that my hands had wrought, and on the labour that I had laboured to do: and, behold, all was vanity and vexation of spirit, and there was no profit under the sun" (Ecclesiastes 2:10–11).

Me and My Shadow

One of the greatest thinkers of the early church, Bishop Augustine of Hippo (354–430), eloquently described our nature in his great treatise *City of God*. While discussing the spiritual orientation that determines whether one is a citizen of "the city of God" or "the city of Man," Augustine coined the Latin phrase *incurvatus in se*, by which he referred to the human soul's tendency to "curve into itself": to become primarily interested in or even obsessed with its own desires and interests. Augustine believed and taught that as humans

> Incurvatus in se: *Latin expression coined by St. Augustine, meaning, "curved into oneself"*

we are created to think about ourselves; self-love is hard-wired into us by our Creator.

However, Augustine made the important distinction that we cannot love ourselves properly by giving ourselves first place in all things.

Instead, the proper love of self proceeds from loving God first and placing His will for our lives above our own. This is how we were meant to live, and it is, according to Augustine, the only path to genuine peace and blessedness. Perhaps the most famous saying that Augustine used to illustrate this point is found in his other great work, *Confessions*, where he said, "You have made us for yourself, O Lord, and our heart is restless until it rests in you."[3]

Centuries later, Martin Luther (significantly, an Augustine monk when he was still a part of the Roman Catholic Church) picked up on Bishop Augustine's line of reasoning

---

[3] Augustine, *Confessions*, ed. David Vincent Meconi, Ignatius Critical Editions (San Francisco: Ignatius Press), bk. 1,1–2,2.5,5: CSEL 33, 1–5.

and carried it much further. In fact, Luther saved much of his most scathing language about the human tendency toward spiritual navel-gazing for those who take one of God's greatest gifts to humanity—the church—and pervert it to their own, selfish ends. Luther's harsh words for this particular manifestation of *incurvatus in se* was motivated by what he saw as the church's apostasy and greed, demonstrated, in Luther's view, by the corruption-riddled practice of selling indulgences—essentially, licenses to sin—and other techniques used by the Roman Catholic clergy of Luther's day to raise money.

Luther loudly condemned such practices as "works righteousness." In his classic *Commentary on Romans*, he rails against any human attempt to achieve righteousness apart from the grace of God, freely bestowed in Jesus Christ.[4]

Luther wrote, "Our nature has been so deeply curved in upon itself because of the viciousness of original sin that it not only turns the finest gifts of God in upon itself and enjoys them . . . indeed, it even uses God himself to achieve these aims, but it also seems to be ignorant to this very fact."[5] In other words, we are deeply prone, not only to worship God's gifts instead of God, but also to see God himself as our own, private benefactor. In "selfie theology," God is the heavenly goose whose only job is to keep laying the golden eggs. Tragically, we can be guilty of such idolatrous

---

[4] Jacob Preus, *Works of Martin Luther*, vol. 25, *Lectures on Romans* (St. Louis: Concordia, 1972), 260.

[5] Ibid., 291.

and self-magnifying thinking without even realizing it. The church itself has struggled to resist the siren call of selfie culture—when the church gives in, its witness in the world is only further diminished.

The Gospel about Me

It is always the church's mission to bring the gospel of Jesus Christ to the world, but even that seemingly simple call is fraught with complexity. Chiefly, the American church has struggled to balance its desire to faithfully share the gospel with a perceived need to retain cultural relevance in an environment guided less and less by a traditional Christian worldview. Unfortunately, we have too often allowed ourselves to conform to the pattern of this world rather than boldly proclaim a different way.

As mentioned earlier, I was senior pastor of a large, growing, and suburban church for more than thirty years. I am totally sympathetic with the difficult circumstances of the American church today. We have a message to be proclaimed, which is the central task of the church. Most every ordained leader I know has been deeply touched by the Lord and sincerely called to proclaim, in word and deed, the good news.

But there is also a church to be led, people to be ministered to, programs to be run, and energy to be harnessed. What is most important? What programs really work? What does "work" really mean in a church, anyway? To attract and retain membership, leaders assess the programs—youth and children's programs, sermon topics, worship music, and even décor—that are most likely to appeal to the current congregation and prospective members. In other words, consumerism is alive and well in today's church. I freely admit that this is a sincere dilemma for every church leader to face.

But in much of our conversation about the dangers of consumerism within the church, we have failed to acknowledge that a consumer mind-set is only a symptom of this broader modern egocentrism—selfie theology—that sees all things as valuable only in relationship to the individual self. What makes this so perplexing for church leaders is the temptation this poses to anyone wanting to grow his or her church.

The tempting whisper is in every pastor's ear almost every day: if you want to reach them, make the gospel all about them.

This is why the subject of generosity is so vexing for most pastors; it focuses the dilemma. As a pastor, am I to comfort the afflicted or afflict the comfortable? Often, we choose simply to ignore the subject altogether. Even when it is discussed, we have no relevant language for it except the same self-centeredness of our culture—everyone is entitled to pick and choose where, when, and how we will support the ongoing work of the gospel. As a result, giving becomes—like everything else—only valuable when it suits our self-determined preferences and beliefs.

> *The tempting whisper is in every pastor's ear almost every day: if you want to reach them, make the gospel all about them.*

My Best Buy

In this connection, I have a rather embarrassing story to relate. My wife, Fran, and I frequently travel on weekends and attend whatever congregation is in the community. It has long been our custom to put aside money for our tithe in a separate account so that when we are in attendance at a particular church on Sunday, we can put a check for our contribution in the offering plate when it is passed. Not too long ago, we were attending Sunday worship in the town where we were visiting, and when the plate was passed, we put in a check for $800, which was the amount in our account that we had purposed for our tithe.

After the service, we happened to be on an errand to the local Best Buy. I confess to being enamored of the latest gadget, and while I was in the store, looking for a replacement thumb drive or some other such thing, I noticed that Best Buy had a special promotion for the latest high-definition, flat-screen television. I could hardly believe my eyes when I saw that they were offering a TV that would usually cost well in excess of $1,000 for a mere $800!

And then, I got to thinking . . . *Eight hundred . . . That's a really good price for this TV! And that's about the same as the check I just wrote in church . . . I wonder if I could go back there and ask them to give me back my check? Then, I could . . .*

Yes, that's right! I was actually considering the idea of stopping payment on my church contribution check so I could buy the nice, shiny, new TV! Clearly, even career pastors are not immune to the seductions of the secular mind-set!

My ethical struggle in Best Buy illustrates the broader truth: in the secular age, many people are more interested in what they can *get* from church—what it can do for them—than in what they can offer to others. Instead of giving ourselves as what Paul described as a "living sacrifice" (Romans 12:1), all too often, in the words attributed to evangelist D. L. Moody, we keep "crawling off the altar." In my case, I was crawling toward that new TV.

But enough about me . . .

 KEY POINTS

- We live in an increasingly self-centered, secular age.

- This is more than a cultural phenomenon; it affects our hearts and souls.

- In an effort to win followers, the church has given in to this self-centeredness.

- The church must resist the momentum of present culture to recover its kingdom mission.

QUESTIONS FOR DISCUSSION

1. Did selfie theology start with the millennial generation and the advent of social media? When else have we seen this "inward curve"?

2. What are some moments or environments in your own life in which you feel the pressure of this worldview? In what ways have you given in to the tyranny of the self?

3. How have you seen churches emulate the narratives of self-centeredness in the broader culture?

4. Based on your own observation, have churches been successful when they have tried to appeal to people using selfie theology? How would you measure that success?

CHAPTER 2

COUNTERCULTURAL GENEROSITY

———•———

On the end table by the reading chair in my study is a stack of books that would confuse any librarian. I have a Bible, a book of sermons by a preacher from two centuries ago, a historical novel, a book on household plumbing (we've had issues), a spy novel, a book on Christian leadership, and an owner's manual for a new camera, which, like most owner's manuals in my house, remains unread. But there is one more book that has helped me think afresh about the message of our Lord and his church: a very unlikely source of fresh insight. I am sure the author never had the church or a church leader in mind when he wrote it. A friend in the marketing world gave it to me. It is a business book . . . the kind you find at the airport terminal next to the magazines. I've had it on my end table for two years and have read it more than a few times. It has a memorable one-word title: *Zag*.

Its complete title is *Zag: The Number One Strategy of High-Performance Brands* (Berkeley: Riders), and it was released in 2006. In this too-short book, marketing guru Marty Neumeier lays out a basic principle for successful corporate leadership and branding: "When everybody else zigs . . . you need to zag." That is to say, when the current of things is heading one way, go the other. Go against the intuitive message you listen to all the time. Go crosscurrent. Go on a zag against the boring, one-way zigs of the culture. I was intrigued from the moment I opened up the book.

Of course, it is not foolproof by any means. It doesn't try to be that, especially for a church or a body of believers. But what it does do is claim a new direction, a new vision, and a new perspective on life and leadership. In this simple concept, we can hear the faint echo of our Lord's call to us to follow where he leads: against the current of the world. He said to the man zigging off with the crowd to bury his father, "Let the dead bury the dead . . . you, zag your way over with me." To the woman condemned by the zig-minded crowd because of real sin and brokenness, Jesus said, "I do not condemn you!" Wow! That was a new direction! Paul zagged on the road to Damascus and became the greatest advocate for the very church he was commissioned to extinguish. To zag is to be the salt of the earth, the light of the world, and the new wine for a new day.

> *To "zag" is to push back against a culture . . . the church was born to zag!*

The Zag?

It is so simple. It means pushing back against a culture, a market, or an era that is always seeking to pull everything in its wake. From the perspective of the author, companies and businesses need to figure out how they are going to zag: to cut across the grain of the market they seek to dominate. The church was born for this!

In a very zaggy parable, Jesus says that the children of light can learn a thing or two from the shrewd, business-minded children of the world. Be shrewd. Be wise. Be strategic about the future. In a world filled with constant noise, overhyped programming, and sales presentations, we might gain the attention of many if we were quiet, bold, and clear. In a world that is telling everyone to get everything they can get—we give. In a culture filled with new ideas and new ways of having it all, we instead go old-school. The practice of generosity, in a grabby world of gimmes and "got it," is the time-tested way to give the gospel away.

We have every possible motivation to zag in today's world. Not only that, but this countercultural move is coded into the church's DNA; we should be the all-time masters of the art, based on our beginnings and our history. In fact, according to the basic principles of the world we live in, the church should never have survived its first few years. To co-opt the language of the business book, our whole existence is based on the biggest zag in the universe—the life and ministry of Jesus Christ.

The original zag is, of course, the incarnation itself. "While we were still sinners," Paul says famously in Romans 5:8, "Christ . . ." I wonder what that last bit of that seminal verse would say if we were writing it. Did Christ come to scold? Did he excuse? Did he punish? No! Going counter to anything that could have otherwise been expected, he came to save: "Christ died for us"! Any other religion or ruler or authority imaginable would have been different. But Christ came to the world to save the sinner; he loved the sinner; he died for the sinner. That is a zag!

Washing Feet

One of Jesus' most famous actions and lessons came on the last night of his earthly life. Indeed, like so many of the moments and teachings of the last week of his life, the washing of his disciples' feet makes clear the centrality of what it means to give up.

Our familiarity with Jesus' actions that night, along with the intervening centuries of church tradition, have dulled us to the incalculable impact Jesus must have had on his disciples as they watched him remove his outer clothing, pour water into a bowl, grab a towel, and begin going around the circle, cleaning everyone's feet. In the cultural context of that place and time, to the dumbstruck apostles this would have been something like our watching the president of the United States removing his or her usual business attire and putting on a janitor's jumpsuit, then cleaning the restrooms in an airport.

Foot-washing was a task reserved for the lowest servant in the pecking order. It's not difficult to understand why: take the usual footwear of the day—sandals—and combine them with walking around all day in streets that were not only either dusty or muddy, but also constituted the principal means of getting rid of human and animal waste and other effluvia, and you can imagine what the typical person's feet looked and smelled like by day's end.

And yet, this is the very task that Jesus—the Rabbi, the Master, the miracle-worker who had confounded the temple hierarchy and the crowds alike with his uncompromising, authoritative teaching—took upon himself, only hours before he was taken violently, subjected to the mockery of a trial, and brutally executed by the most painful means available. Rather than girding his loins for what lay ahead, he unwrapped the robe around his waist. Instead of suiting up, he dressed down.

In later days and years, this indelible lesson would only become more powerful in the memories of Jesus' followers. As they thought back on those last hours with their Master, and especially after the promised Holy Spirit quickened their hearts and minds to understand—to really, deeply internalize—all that Jesus had taught them, they could scarcely fail to see that Christ had placed self-sacrificial service— giving up—squarely in the center of his church's mission to the world.

In doing this, Jesus was modeling what lay at the heart of God: what God has always intended for his people to be about. Throughout the Old Testament, we read again and again of God's concern for those in need, coupled with his mandate that his chosen people should share that same preoccupation. In Isaiah 58, God clearly announced through the prophet how he wants his people to display their devotion to him. He wants them "to loose the bonds of wickedness, to undo the straps of the yoke, to let the oppressed go free, and to break every yoke . . . to share your bread with the hungry and bring the homeless poor into your house; when you see the naked, to cover him, and not to hide yourself from your own flesh" (vv. 6–7).

Even more remarkable is the result that God described when his people sacrifice themselves on behalf of others: "Then shall your light break forth like the dawn, and your healing shall spring up speedily; your righteousness shall go before you; the glory of the LORD shall be your rear guard . . . If you pour yourselves out for the hungry and satisfy the desire of the afflicted, then shall your light rise in the darkness and your gloom be as the noonday" (vv. 8–10).

Churches in Need

I do a good deal of church consulting, including what I call "aftermath analysis": I get a call from a pastor asking me to help him untie some knots. The church has seized up; momentum is gone. It isn't reaching new people; its members are tired and apathetic.

I come, listen, and observe. And often what I find is that they are living in the aftermath of something; some trauma has occurred, and they have drawn in on themselves. They have started to focus only on their own membership, the needs of their own families. They have dialed back giving to missions; they have curtailed plans to plant churches. They have pulled away from denominational participation. Like an exhausted mom who cries out, "I need some 'me' time!" as she heads to the mall, churches can say, in effect, "We need some 'we' time!"

When that happens, a "shrinkage spiral" begins. The church *curves in* on itself. It tries overly hard to satisfy its members, to renew and recommit to its core competencies (teaching, reaching, and preaching, but mostly for its members). It is all very normal, natural, and understandable. It is intuitive—but it is a trap. *The more the church looks in on itself, the less it can give of itself; the less it gives of itself, the less of itself there is to give.* And the congregation slides.

In fact, as I hope to show, the counterintuitive action is the hardest to do: to give. To offer up to God whatever can be had; to give *up* to the Lord the best we can bring. In a phrase, *giving up* is the way we can rise up. True, it will require vision and energy and the focus of some of our best thinkers; it will require some very sacrificial acts on the part of many. But the synergy of a generous church, a church fully invested in a mission-facing future, is amazing. As generosity takes root in Christ's church, both the church and the world will feel the full force of a love more powerful than they could have ever imagined.

Could God make any clearer the importance of the willingness of his people to "give up" on behalf of others? Could the resulting impact of such behavior on the rest of the world be any more graphically illustrated? Clearly, a church that wants to get serious about following the Lord Jesus will have to put into practice the principal teaching of its Master. That is precisely what his earliest followers did, and it is to their story that we turn next.

KEY POINTS

- The church cannot achieve its mission by giving in to the forces of culture.

- Sometimes, when everyone else "zigs," you must "zag."

- Generosity is in the DNA of the church, as shown by the life and mission of Jesus.

- "Giving up" was the principal way the first Christians distinguished themselves.

QUESTIONS FOR DISCUSSION

1. What marketing campaigns or cultural phenomena have you seen succeed based on the principle of "zagging"?

2. Other than the passages discussed in the chapter, what were other ways Jesus' life and ministry could be seen as countercultural?

3. What would you describe as the central teaching of Jesus, based on what he says and does in the gospel? How does that relate to the idea of "giving up"?

CHAPTER 3

THE HIDDEN VIRTUE OF
THE EARLY CHURCH

———•———

In his book, *A Secular Age*, philosopher Charles Taylor shows us the development of the secular mind-set in Western society. He explains how we have moved from a culture in which it was almost impossible not to believe in God to one in which religious belief of any kind is simply one viable option among many. Many people (including me) have struggled mightily with the density of his book; I have put the book back on the shelf many times and instead resorted to authors who write *about* Charles Taylor and his book. But sometimes even they confuse the simple truth. For those who wonder what secularism is, I offer my simple, controlling image that is both the icon and idol of this secular age: the selfie.

As suggested in the first chapter, secularism can be described in this new modern word invented for our age. A selfie is a picture of *me* doing something that I want to do. And every selfie I snap has the same theme: *ME . . . enjoying, relishing, and reveling through the pleasures and senses of life, with everything else in the background.*

The early church knew their version of secularism by another ancient name: paganism. By its very nature, paganism is a religion of delights and decadence. Yet, the early church stood apart from this; resisting it. They stood in it, ministering and loving and giving to those in need. Nowhere do we see this more beautifully portrayed than in the writing of the great apostle Paul.

A Legacy of Generosity

In the days of the first church, their number one distinction was exceeding generosity and giving. The miracles of the tongues of fire seen at Pentecost convinced a goodly number of believers to remain confident in the Lord's return. It was convicting. But the most sustaining ministry, it seems, may have been the program of food given for widows and orphans. Indeed, Acts 2 relates that in those earliest days, when many of the first Christians were living as displaced refugees, members of the church pooled their resources to make sure that no one was hungry or lacked a safe place to sleep. Some of them went so far as to voluntarily liquidate their real estate holdings to provide assistance for those who didn't have adequate resources. In Acts 4:32, we read of this community, "Now the full number of those who believed were of one heart and soul, and no one said that any of the things that belonged to him was his own, but they had everything in common."

Paul may be the early church's most famous convert, but he was also one of the most generous in how he gave. The gospel went worldwide because of his tireless work to bring the saving message of Jesus across the (mostly Gentile) Roman Empire. And like Jesus, Paul never seemed concerned with how others perceived him, never seemed to care if he was aligning himself with the dominant cultural narratives of his day.

As Paul wrote his letters to the young churches in Europe and Asia Minor, he consistently emphasized the importance of generosity. In Romans 12:13, in his closing admonitions, he told the Roman Christians, "Contribute to the needs of the saints and seek to show hospitality." In his letter to the church in Ephesus, he urged all the Christians to work at some form of honest employment, "doing honest work with [their] own hands, so that [they] may have something to share with anyone in need" (Ephesians 4:28). As he imparted his pastoral wisdom to his young apprentice Timothy, he advised the young evangelist to instruct his converts "to do good, to be rich in good works, to be generous and ready to share" (1 Timothy 6:18). Clearly, Paul was shaping the features and virtues of the early church. Generosity, open-handedness, giving, and sharing were being hard-wired into the consciousness of the earliest Christians.

Clearly, Paul was shaping the features and virtues of the early church. Generosity, open-handedness, giving, and sharing were being hard-wired into the consciousness of the earliest Christians.

A Missing Link

A few years ago, I made a startling discovery about the letters of Paul: he never mentioned the earthly ministry of our Lord, with one or two notable exceptions. I had always known that there was a very strange disconnect between the written words of the apostle Paul and the spoken word and actions of our Lord. Of all the miracles, messages, actions, healings, and encounters that the Lord had, the chief spokesman and strategist of the New Testament didn't mention even one of them. Paul would have known of these stories, of course. Luke and Mark were traveling companions with the evangelist; he would have heard plenty from those two. Most students of the Bible notice this fact and find it interesting. Some find it provocative. But it is clear that Paul knew about Jesus, mentioned him many times, understood that he was the Lord of history, who had come during the reign of Pontius Pilate (1 Timothy 6:13).

But there is an intersection between Paul and Jesus on one topic. Generosity. Other than quoting Jesus' words at the Last Supper (in 1 Corinthians 11), Paul only refers to the actual words of Jesus twice. And in both cases, Paul's focus is on generosity.

The first case occurs in 2 Corinthians 9, when Paul is exhorting the Corinthian Christians to generosity, in large part by presenting the example of the Macedonian churches. In fact, in the New International translation of 2 Corinthians 9, the word "generous" or "generosity" occurs five times. Beginning in verse 6, Paul lays out for the Corinthians the case for generosity:

> The point is this: whoever sows sparingly will also reap sparingly, and whoever sows bountifully will also reap bountifully. Each one must give as he has

decided in his heart, not reluctantly or under compulsion, for God loves a cheerful giver. And God is able to make all grace abound to you, so that having all sufficiency in all things at all times, you may abound in every good work. . . .

He who supplies seed to the sower and bread for food will supply and multiply your seed for sowing and increase the harvest of your righteousness. You will be enriched in every way to be generous in every way, which through us will produce thanksgiving to God. (2 Corinthians 9:6–11)

Why did Paul select the particular imagery of seed and bread? I believe the answer is in Luke 6, where Jesus says, "Give, and it will be given to you. Good measure, pressed down, shaken together, running over, will be put into your lap. For with the measure you use it will be measured back to you" (Luke 6:38). As Paul admonished the Corinthians toward generosity, he provided what might be considered one of the earliest commentaries on Jesus' words as found in Luke's gospel. Paul was echoing Jesus!

The second instance is much later in Paul's ministry, as reported in Acts 20, during Paul's tearful farewell address to the Ephesian elders.

And now I commend you to God and to the word of his grace, which is able to build you up and to give you the inheritance among all those who are sanctified. I coveted no one's silver or gold or apparel.

You yourselves know that these hands ministered to my necessities and to those who were with me. In all things I have shown you that by working hard in this way we must help the weak and remember the words of the Lord Jesus, how he himself said, "It is more blessed to give than to receive." (vv. 32–35)

Do you know what is perhaps the most interesting thing about the words of Jesus as Paul quoted them here? They do not appear in any of the gospels! Of course, there was a rich tradition of "sayings of Jesus" that circulated actively among the earliest Christians, though they were never written down. Today, we might think of them as "memes." Imagine that! There was a meme in the early church from the sayings of Jesus that was so pervasive and so omnipresent in the culture of the New Testament church that Paul knew it himself, remembered it, quoted it, and admonished the believers in Ephesus to remember it as well.

Perhaps the most pervasive "meme" in the early church was Jesus' saying: "It is more blessed to give than to receive."

When I considered these two instances, I came to this compelling conclusion: there were many virtues and values in the early church that set it apart from the Roman Empire. But the single most pervasive attitude that was shared, accepted, taught, practiced, and encouraged might have been the one that is kept out of sight today: generosity. This quality appears to have been everywhere in the early church. It was like an atmospheric condition of the first Christians. It pervaded everything they did.

The Focus of the Church

We can say this much about the early Christians: their church grew beyond the imagination of most church leaders today. But it wasn't because of some coordinated marketing plan they developed. It seems to me that they weren't primarily motivated by a desire to garner numbers, attention, or followers—or even, as we might say today, "likes." But what we do know is that they were radically sure of their identity as followers of Christ; taking their cue from what they saw him doing, they did likewise.

It wasn't their strategy to stand out, yet I believe it was the radical way they cared for one another, even to the point of giving away their own possessions, that made these new believers different from the society that surrounded them. Instead of finding their security in the usual sources—money, influence, or power—they placed their ultimate hope in the promises of the risen Christ, only visible through the eyes of faith. Their reliance on the One who taught and displayed sacrificial love made them different, placing the rest of society on notice that this was a group of people who did not operate according to the usual assumptions. By imitating their Lord in loving each other unconditionally and sacrificially, those first Jesus followers zagged . . . and the world has never been the same.

The life of Jesus, the ministry of Paul, the work of the church in Acts—all of this attracted attention in ancient society. Why? Because it was obvious that such behavior did not proceed from any ordinary, human source. No philosophy, no other form of religious belief, had ever produced a movement that, despite its apparent lack of any political, military, or social base, could endure and even flourish in the face of organized opposition from those in power. The followers of Jesus were willing to give and then to keep on giving. And the world responded to the magnetic pull of their unselfish authenticity. As God described in Isaiah 58:8, they shone like a brilliant searchlight in a dark, selfish world.

 KEY POINTS

- The pressure toward an egocentric secularism can feel overwhelming.

- Paul's message of generosity was a pointedly different narrative from that of the dominant Roman culture.

- Paul uniquely singled out Jesus' teaching on generosity and urged his churches to put his words into action.

- The countercultural message of generosity didn't leave the church irrelevant—it garnered attention and followers as a result.

DISCUSSION QUESTIONS

1. What shifts have you noticed in culture and institutions over the course of your life? How have you seen the momentum of secular individualism alter the landscape?

2. How have you noticed individuals or communities try to push back against some of this momentum?

3. Other than the saying of Jesus that Paul chose to quote, what other teachings from Jesus would you have guessed Paul might have focused on instead?

4. What was Paul's plan for evangelism in the early church? How does it differ from most evangelism strategies in today's churches?

CHAPTER 4

GENEROSITY AS EVANGELISM: A CASE STUDY

———•———

When we think about evangelism, we are usually imagining people knocking on doors or handing out tracts. We think of revival tents and red-faced, passionate preachers leading the masses to walk down the aisle and come to the Lord. If we are thinking more recently, maybe we are picturing a welcoming committee at our church or a community outreach team. We probably also think about things as pragmatic as the graphic design work on our website, published sermon titles, and the curb appeal of our worship space or facility.

The church has not ignored evangelism—far from it. At the heart of almost every church I have visited is a focus on reaching more people in everything they do. Yet, for all the energy and thought that's invested, most churches overlook the single most impactful channel for evangelism: generosity. Looking at the church's actions in its earliest days, and seeing the secular culture's response could open a channel of gospel presentation to an unbelieving world that could reach many more people. In this real case study, the generosity of the church made the Christian faith truly believable . . . and tangible.

Deadly Plagues and a Living Church

During the second century, Rome was a huge city, swarming with people. So imagine that city in the grip of a deadly plague, centuries before the discovery of antibiotics or even modern sanitation.

Such was the situation in Rome in AD 165. After an initial outbreak among Roman troops engaged in the siege of Seleucia, a Persian city on the Tigris River, the disease, believed by many scholars to have been smallpox, spread rapidly to Gaul and the Rhine provinces, carried there by infected Roman legions. The fourth-century historian Flavius Eutropius asserted that huge swaths of the population of the Roman Empire succumbed to the deadly pestilence.[1]

The Greek physician Galen, who traveled to Rome from his home in Asia Minor at the request of the authorities, described symptoms such as fever, diarrhea, swollen throats, and skin eruptions. Some estimates place the death toll during the fifteen years of the plague at perhaps five million, killing as much as a third of the population in some areas and devastating the Roman army.

The cities of the ancient world were fearfully susceptible to the spread of diseases. They were dreadfully overcrowded, with nearly nonexistent sewer systems; human urine and excrement were dumped in the streets and often contaminated the public water supply. There were no screens on windows, so flies and other vermin had free access, not only to the filth

---

[1] Eutropius, *Breviarium historiae Romanae*, XXXI, 6.24

in the streets, but also to human food stores. Under such conditions, a disease such as smallpox or measles, to which much of the population had no previous exposure or immunity, might run through a city like wildfire.

In the face of the onslaught from such a fearful, invisible, and unstoppable enemy, many Romans chose the most obvious solution: they ran. They understood that they needed to be as far away from those infected as possible. Often, they left behind sick or dying family members or household slaves. Sometimes, the suffering wretches were even dragged out of their homes and dumped on the street by those desperate to avoid infection. Contemporary writers report scores of unburied dead, simply left to decompose or become food for scavenging beasts. It wasn't that the people were callous—they simply had no imagination for another solution.

The group that stood in starkest contrast to the panicked public was the Christians. Eusebius, an early church leader and historian, wrote of those days that "[the Christians] tended to the dying and their burial, countless numbers with no one to care for them. Others gathered together from all parts of the city a multitude of those withered from famine and distributed bread to them all."[2] Rather than fleeing to save themselves, the followers of Jesus stayed in Rome and other cities of the empire, risking their own health and, in many cases, dying, in order to take care of the sick and dying—whether the sufferers were Christians or not.

---

[2] Eusebius, *Church History*, trans. Paul Meier (Grand Rapids, Kregel, 2007), 293.

Some scholars believe that the compassionate efforts of these early Christians even worked to reduce the ultimate death toll. Simply by helping sick people stay hydrated and as nourished as possible, they likely prevented a number of people from dying. Also, the therapeutic benefits of a caring presence are well-known. Thus, it seems likely that through a combination of their loving compassion and such simple nursing aids as they could provide, the Christians of the second century saved perhaps thousands of lives that would have otherwise been lost.

But the important thing to note is that the glaring disparity between the behavior of the Christians and that of the surrounding culture did not go unnoticed. As they comforted and nursed back to health those who, perhaps only the day before, would gladly have reported them to the authorities for their "subversive" faith, they demonstrated a quiet courage that defied explanation. As they buried the dead, whom everyone else was afraid to touch, they placed on bold display the ethic of self-sacrificial love that they had learned from their Lord. And when, to the wondering inquiries of their pagan beneficiaries, they answered in one of the "memes" that permeated the early church, "It is more blessed to give than to receive," they established countless beachheads for the gentle conquest of an entire civilization.

Look How They Love

Fast-forward about a century. Sometime near Easter, AD 250, another virulent outbreak raged out of Ethiopia, overtook Egypt, and spread to Rome, Greece, and Syria. Bishop Cyprian of Carthage, who described the appalling symptoms and suffering that accompanied the plague, remarked that it seemed likely that the world was coming to an end. At its height the Plague of Cyprian, as it has come to be called, claimed the lives of some five thousand people daily in Rome.

However, as with the Antonine Plague a century earlier, this new, worldwide calamity provided yet another opportunity for the body of Christ to offer a vivid demonstration of its central ethic of self-sacrifice. As opposed to the pagans, whose priests and leaders had no explanation for the plague other than some vague notion of "the punishment of the gods," Christians possessed a faith in the Resurrection that permitted them to face death with a sense of peace—even joy. Additionally, as they once again ministered to pagans and fellow believers alike, they showed an astounded world an unforgettable image of unconditional love. The witness of the Christians' inexplicable generosity propelled the reputation of the church throughout the Roman world.

General admiration of the Christians for their generosity even made a grudging fan of a hostile Roman emperor. Julian the Apostate (ruled AD 361–363) is noted for his attempts to revive the "old-time religion" of Greek polytheism in order to return the empire to what he saw as its "traditional values."

But Julian had a problem: the Christians were too well-known for their charity. Julian thought to stem the popularity of Christianity by establishing a competing "pagan" system of philanthropy throughout the empire. But somehow, his government-sponsored program failed to catch on. He complained of this in a letter he wrote in AD 362, addressed to Arsacius, a high priest of the Greek religion, who lived in Galatia:

> The religion of the Greeks does not yet prosper as I would wish, on account of those who profess it. . . . Why then do we think that this is sufficient and do not observe how the kindness of Christians to strangers, their care for the burial of their dead, and the sobriety of their lifestyle has done the most to advance their cause?
>
> . . . For it is disgraceful when no Jew is a beggar and the impious Galileans [the name given by Julian to Christians] support our poor in addition to their own; everyone is able to see that our coreligionists are in want of aid from us. Teach also those who profess the Greek religion to contribute to such services, and the villages of the Greek religion to offer the first-fruits to the gods. Accustom those of the Greek religion to such benevolence, teaching them that this has been our work from ancient times.[3]

Poor Emperor Julian! His attempts to impose generosity by decree just couldn't compete with the innate generosity for

---

[3] Edward J. Chinnock, *A Few Notes on Julian and a Translation of His Public Letters* (London: David Nutt, 1901), 75–78, as quoted in D. Brendan Nagle and Stanley M. Burstein, *The Ancient World: Readings in Social and Cultural History* (Englewood Cliffs, NJ: Prentice Hall, 1995), 314–15.

which the Christians were already famous! As history demonstrates, Julian's attempts to revive Greco-Roman polytheism ultimately came to naught; Christianity continued its steady progression among the minds and hearts of the people of the Roman Empire. In 363, when Julian died in battle, his campaign to reestablish Hellenic polytheism died with him. Christianity would have no more serious rivals in the Mediterranean world until the rise of Islam, beginning in AD 610.

The love that Christians showed is a principal reason for the ascendancy of the early church.

Without question, the love that Christians showed for one another and for their pagan neighbors is a principal reason for the ascendancy of the church, even in the face of official persecution. Tertullian, writing in the last years of the second century, famously contrasted the behaviors by which Christians and pagans were known:

"'Look,' [the pagans] say, 'how [the Christians] love one another' (for they themselves hate one another); 'and how they are ready to die for each other' (for they themselves are readier to kill each other)."[4]

Case Study Analysis

What do we see from this case study of these Roman plagues? We may notice four things.

First, we see the attitudes of the prevailing culture. The Romans who left were operating according to the cause that

---

[4] Tertullian, *Apologeticus*, ch. 39, sec. 7.

their society prized above all: self-preservation. At the end of the day, the Romans believed that you had to leave behind the suffering in order to save yourself. Some might even have claimed to be operating in the public interest. The Roman politician Cicero had coined the phrase *salus populi suprema lex esto* ("Let the safety of the people be the highest law"). Roman citizens could tell themselves that to stay behind and help would risk further exposure of others to the disease. They were being virtuous—even heroic!—by separating themselves from those who were afflicted.

Second, we see that the Christian response worked in opposition to the prevailing culture and exposed the brokenness of its narrative. The disciples of Christ didn't wait to hear what the public stance on the issue was. They didn't run any focus groups to see what course of action would lead to the most publicity. Their actions were prompted solely by the mission of the kingdom of God, seen in the example of Jesus Christ. So, while the Romans may have been soothing themselves with their maxims about the common good, seeing Christians risk their own lives to give a proper burial to the very men and women they had left to die short-circuited any superficial belief they had in their system.

Third, we see that from the Christian response, the surrounding culture had a clear image of who the church was and what it stood for. Christians had been known as a quirky, potentially dangerous sect. They did not participate in many aspects of Roman culture and were thought to hold bizarrely conservative views on sexuality. But after receiving the incredible generosity of Christians during the plagues, the Romans added a new dimension to their image of Christians. They understood that inwardly—within the church—they held one another to a strict moral code, and outwardly they were self-sacrificial and loving. Tim Keller, in a typically memorable way, described the first Christians: "The early church was strikingly different from the culture around it in this way—the pagan society was stingy with its money and promiscuous with its body. A pagan gave nobody their money and practically gave everybody their body. And the Christians came along and gave practically nobody their body and gave practically everybody their money."[5]

That difference surely wasn't lost on the Romans who were observing the Christians.

Fourth, the surrounding culture began to emulate the Christians' way of living. Take a moment to reflect on the evangelical implications of this: the generosity of the early Christians was so winsome and compelling that the emperor of the Roman Empire demanded (unsuccessfully) that his religious authorities attempt to replicate their model.

Public Relations

We have discussed the first two observations at some length in the previous chapters. Hopefully, it's clear enough by now that the call of the church is to resist the temptation to give

---

[5] As quoted in Bryan Patterson, "A Remarkable Shift in Cultural Christianity," *Melbourne Herald-Sun*, September 15, 2012, Sunday edition.

in to the selfie theology that surrounds us and instead offer a radically alternative message of generosity. In doing so, the church will demonstrate the ultimate insufficiency of the dominant belief systems and show that, in fact, giving up, as seen in the life, death, and resurrection of Jesus, reflects the most viable, fully realized vision for human flourishing.

Our interest here lies in the third observation. The generous response of Christians led the surrounding culture to a clear understanding of the church's beliefs. They observed that Christians held one another to a strict and counter-cultural moral code, and they saw the radical, self-emptying love that they had for those outside their fellowship.

So, with that said, here's a tough question: What is our present culture's impression of the church?

I'm afraid the answer is often not very flattering. A 2014 Pew Research study of people who, though religious at one time, now identify themselves with no organized religious group, revealed the following reasons given for leaving their faith:

- "Religion focuses on power and politics."
- "Organized religious groups are more divisive than uniting."
- "Too many Christians doing un-Christian things."
- "Religion is not a religion anymore; it's a business, all about money."[6]

---

[6] Michael Lipka, "Why America's 'Nones' Left Religion Behind." *Fact Tank* (Pew Research Center blog), August 24, 2016, http://www.pewresearch.org /fact-tank/2016/08/24/why-americas-nones-left-religion-behind/.

Similarly, in 2013, the Barna Group, in cooperation with the Cornerstone Knowledge Network, conducted a nationwide survey of people aged eighteen to twenty-nine: the generation popularly called "millennials," a demographic currently abandoning the church in record numbers. Factors for this massive departure from the church, as uncovered by the research, included the following:

- The church prioritizes relevancy over authenticity.
- The church's messaging is unclear.
- The church values activity over piety.
- The church does not personify the teachings of Christ.
- The church does not do enough to build caring, mentoring communities.[7]

There's a lot we could unpack here, but when we boil it down, we find a disturbing inversion of the early church's image in the world. They were known for their internal discipline and morality—we are seen as judging everyone else's behavior while ignoring our own. They were known for their outward generosity—we are seen as more interested in spending within our private club. If it is a battle for hearts and minds, the sad truth is, we're losing.

---

[7] Barna Group and Cornerstone Knowledge Network, *Making Space for Millennials* (Ventura, CA: Barna Group, n.d.), cited in Marian V. Liautaud, "5 Things Millennials Wish the Church Would Be," Exponential website, https://exponential.org/5-things-millennials-wish-the-church-would-be/, accessed May 7, 2017.

It isn't as if we aren't trying: quite the opposite. As discussed, we've created evangelism programs in our churches specifically tasked with telling our communities who we are and what we are about.

But what if that's the problem?

The early church didn't seem interested in evangelism as an isolated program. They weren't primarily invested in understanding their target audience and crafting a message that would be likely to impact them. It seems that the first concern of the early church was following the footsteps of Jesus and living out his message of loving sacrificially, of giving up. Is that a strategy for evangelism that could work for us?

Let me rephrase that: If your plan to evangelize your community was so impactful that national leaders went out of their way to copy your strategies, would you consider that a success? And the truth is that the early church's missions of mercy and love were *not* calculated to be strategic at all. I doubt seriously that church leaders thought in terms of public image or strategic mission. They were simply doing what came naturally, or rather, supernaturally, and it impressed and moved the hearts of others.

Reaching Out by Giving Up

Indeed, behavior like that of the early Christians was impossible for the surrounding society to ignore. For those accustomed to the need to fiercely defend themselves against all comers and weighted down by the constant realization that no one would come to their aid if they became incapacitated, the self-giving attitudes and actions of the followers of Jesus had almost the appearance of a miracle. How could human beings behave this way? What motivated such behavior that ran counter to all expectations?

We don't define ourselves in the hearts and minds of others through propaganda or rhetoric. We certainly won't define ourselves by judging and condemning those we hope to reach. The testimony of the early church is that we can only redefine ourselves in the eyes of the world through unexpected, unprecedented generosity. The response from the survivors of these plagues was gratitude, and—as the French proverb puts it—"gratitude is the heart's memory." The radical generosity of early Christians stunned the Romans into gratitude and in doing so left an indelible image of the gospel etched on every heart.

This is what Jesus did to his hearers in telling the story of the good Samaritan. His audience was so stunned at the shocking generosity of a Samaritan (a sworn enemy of the Jews) that one among them confessed that, more than a priest and more than a Levite, the Samaritan was the one to be admired and emulated.

The only way that humans can have their thinking so radically altered is by the acquisition of a new mind: "the mind of Christ" (1 Corinthians 2:16). Only the Spirit of the One who emptied himself and volunteered for the place of a servant could animate such counterintuitive generosity in the spirits of humankind. And just as counterintuitively, it is this surrender that results in Christ's ultimate victory. Hear the apostle Paul's hymn to the Philippian church: "Therefore God has highly exalted him and bestowed on him the name that is above every name" (Philippians 2:9).

Clearly, the church gains the most when it gives up the most. Rodney Stark, in his influential book *The Rise of Christianity: How the Obscure, Marginal Jesus Movement Became the Dominant Religious Force in the Western World in a Few Centuries*, argues persuasively that Christianity succeeded, despite its beginnings in a hostile environment, because it offered things that the surrounding society desperately wanted: hope for a better future; an ethic founded upon respect for others; and, perhaps most important, a community of people who cared for one another out of sincere generosity. To the extent that the earliest Christians matched their Lord's prime identifier—"By this all people will know that you are my disciples, if you have love for one another" (John 13:35)—they served as the most convincing argument in favor of their way of living.

Rodney Stark's quote is worth repeating here at length:

Christianity served as a revitalization movement that arose in response to the misery, chaos, fear, and brutality of life in the urban Greco-Roman world. . . . Christianity revitalized life in Greco-Roman cities by providing new norms and new kinds of social relationships able to cope with many urgent problems. To cities filled with the homeless and impoverished, Christianity offered charity as well as hope. To cities filled with newcomers and strangers, Christianity offered an immediate basis for attachment. To cities filled with orphans and widows, Christianity provided a new and expanded sense of family. To cities torn by violent ethnic strife, Christianity offered a new basis for social solidarity. And to cities faced with epidemics, fire, and earthquakes, Christianity offered effective nursing services. . . . For what they brought was not simply an urban movement, but a new culture capable of making life in Greco-Roman cities more tolerable.[8]

In *What If Jesus Had Never Been Born?* D. James Kennedy and Jerry Newcombe note the many ways that Christ and his church have bettered humanity. They argue that on a host of fronts, from civil liberties to the arts, Christianity has transformed the world in overwhelmingly positive ways. Near the end of the book, they underline the central, sacrificial ethic that Christ weaves throughout the fabric of this eternal fellowship: "The great secret of life is not to get but to give. In the final analysis, when you look back over all your life, it will be in those moments of selfless giving, in humble bestowal upon others, that you will see that life has taken on its true significance. Compared with all other things, love stands out as the greatest."[9]

Katrina (A Modern Case Study)

In 2005, Hurricane Katrina and the associated flooding and aftermath knocked out the Ninth Ward in New Orleans.

---

[8] Rodney Stark, *The Rise of Christianity* (Princeton, NJ: Princeton University Press, 1996), 161.

[9] D. James Kennedy and Jerry Newcombe, *What If Jesus Had Never Been Born? The Positive Impact of Christianity in History* (Nashville: Thomas Nelson, 2005), 244.

The political issues that took up a lot of media attention drew the focus away from the work of many churches all around the nation. But there were many relief efforts that were begun by unpaid, inexperienced, but deeply generous people. Here is one such story, as I recall, from Christ Church in Plano.

As happened with a number of churches around the state of Texas, refugees from New Orleans showed up at our doors within a day of the storm. We were hosting weekly dinners at the church already, so we invited them to join us. When we learned that they were staying at a couple of local hotels, we organized our parishioners to provide dinner for them at the hotels for the next couple of weeks. We also worked with the city to set up furnishings in multiple apartments. At one point, we purchased a semitruck–load of mattresses from a manufacturer and distributed them out of our parking lot. We also set up a series of grief ministry dinners to help these weary, bruised folks adjust to the reality of what had happened to them. And, of course, we invited them to come and worship with us. Some are still with us today.

But soon, it became apparent that some of us were going to need to go to New Orleans and provide boots-on-the-ground assistance. I called a friend and member of our church, named Matt, the day after Katrina made landfall.

"This is bad, Matt. The situation as I see it now in the news is dire. I am hearing that churches are struggling to coordinate their relief. I think we have an enormous need here, and I think something needs to be done." That is about all the vision I had for the task that lay ahead of us. The massive storm, the terrible water damage, the human dramas emerging, and the governmental infighting created an atmosphere of confusion and bewilderment.

Four hours later, Matt called me on his cell phone. "I'm on it, David. I'm a few more hours from the flooded area, and they are expecting me by supper. I called ahead and told them that I was bringing food and supplies. Before too much longer, I'll stop and pick up as many buckets of chicken as I can fit in the back of my car."

"What? Matt, you are where?" I was stunned. I had heard and seen reports of a mass exodus out of the city. I hadn't heard that anyone was driving *into* the floods. "What are you *doing*?"

Matt told me that he had to see for himself and find out how to serve. He'd give a full report in the morning. I asked him about his provisions, what he was going to do, and where he would sleep. But Matt, I would come to find out, was a single-minded leader. He ignored my question and continued by reading his shopping list of supplies.

"So here is what I think I need: twenty gallons of water, a couple hundred of rolls of paper towels, toilet paper, bags and bags of diapers, and a few boxes of granola bars. I think we need a fax machine, a printer, a folding table, three chairs, and a few boxes of printer paper."

"Matt, where do you think you'll find all of that stuff? It's going to get pretty sparse the closer you get to New Orleans."

"Oh, I don't need to stop. That's what I have in the back of my SUV. The only stop I need to make is for the buckets of chicken." He paused for a moment and then started to say good-bye. "David, I see a sign for the Colonel coming up. I'm going to get off and get the food. We can talk later." And he was gone.

I was stunned. Matt had paid for every supply out of his own pocket. He would never ask for anything back. But that was just the start of the outpouring from our church to the people of the Ninth Ward in New Orleans.

Over the next twenty-four months, our church sent dozens of mission workers, hundreds of thousands of dollars, relief aid, interns, youth workers, youth groups, along with hundreds of gloves, hammers, boxes, Bibles, good news tracts, and more. It was a full-scale, parish-wide mobilization effort that galvanized the members of Christ Church in a way I had never seen. Whole housefuls of furniture were given to the church to send back with the refugees who returned to New Orleans. Our church, in one single Sunday morning offering, raised more than $90,000 for direct relief of the people of the Ninth Ward. And for years afterwards, many of the people who came to worship and then join Christ Church knew of us because of that extraordinary time of generosity.

This is not unusual—or at least, it shouldn't be. Churches step into a human need with acts of love and generosity because we follow a Lord who stepped into our need. As he healed and touched and restored and comforted, churches everywhere do the same—every day.

In many instances, church participation and its generous acts of mercy and money offering are not reported in the press. Frankly, Christians are the unsung heroes of many efforts to salvage property, lives, marriage, families, and neighborhoods. And it is as natural an act as breathing for most believers. In fact, for the early church it *was* breathing; it was life!

My point is this: What would it be like if the church began to see their efforts at justice, mercy, and generosity and their efforts at widespread evangelistic programs as one and the same thing? This is true giving up: surrendering to the great cause of Christ to love, uphold, save, and bless the hurting and lost people of this world. This is the great secret of the early church: as they gave up to the Lord, people came in to the church. When you place the generous love of Christ at the heart of your ministry, you not only discover the irresistible force it exerts on those around you; you find that your own soul is formed in the process as well.

KEY POINTS

- The plagues in the Roman Empire during the second and third centuries brought the self-sacrificial generosity of Christians to the attention of the surrounding society.

- The Christians' gracious behavior toward friend and foe alike became a principal argument in favor of their faith.

- By surrendering themselves in service, the Christians of the second and third centuries won the battle for the hearts and minds of the Roman Empire.

- Despite its heightened focus on evangelism, the church of the twenty-first century—in contrast to the early church—is failing to clearly communicate its mission.

- Only by placing self-sacrificial love at the core of its identity can the church recover its image in the eyes of the world.

QUESTIONS FOR DISCUSSION

1. If an epidemic, such as Ebola, were to break out where you live, how do you think you would react? Why do you think the Christians of the first and second centuries reacted as they did?

2. What are the main obstacles to self-sacrificial behavior today?

3. In your opinion, do most people hold views of the church similar to those indicated in the presented research? Why do you think this is so?

4. How does your church do evangelism? How could those strategies be transformed by focusing instead on generosity?

CHAPTER 5

GENEROSITY:
THE NEW DISCIPLESHIP

———•———

According to Suzanne Kingsbury, who blogs about books and writing for *Huffington Post*, "our nation has a sort of embarrassing and very consuming addiction: self-help books." She went on to cite *Forbes* for the fact that each year, Americans spend some $11 billion on self-help books.[1]

With a market that size, naturally, Kingsbury had ten top picks to recommend for summer reading in 2016. Her selected titles ranged from Bob Litwin's *Live the Best Story of Your Life* to Sarah Knight's crassly titled *The Life-Changing Magic of Not Giving a* [expletive deleted]. Each of the books on Kingsbury's list is geared toward helping readers figure out for themselves how to become, in her words, "thinner, richer, happier, wiser, and just all around a better person." In other words, the titles on the list are aimed at giving us more tips for getting to the head of the class, the front of the line, the corner office. We are obsessed with wanting to be the best and brightest—and each year we spend $11 billion trying to figure out how to do it better!

---

[1] Suzanne Kingsbury, "The Best Self-Help Books for the Summer of 2016," *Huff Post: The Blog*, June 20, 2016, http://www.huffingtonpost.com /suzanne-kingsbury/the-best-selfhelp-books-f_b_10533322.html.

If we were clear-minded about this, we would see the self-help books for what they are: discipleship manuals! These publishers are marketing step-by-step guides for disciples of the secular life: for a newer and more exciting way of living than could ever be imagined! Maybe a fictional title for an ideal self-help manual might read: *My Life—Wow!* The subtitle might say, *How You Can Be Like Me.* And the contents would be filled with topics that highlight some new scientific findings, some standard ideas, anecdotes, suggestions, testimonies, a few motivational promotions, and, of course, a product tie-in. The entire book can be seen as a way of helping the student (the reader) become like the master (the author).

Naturally, those of us who frequent Christian bookstores expect to see on the shelves Christian manuals such as these. Publishers of small group studies, adult education resources, Sunday school materials, and devotional books offer the church and the believer a wide variety of options to choose from. Here again, the intention behind the Christian discipleship curriculum is to help the student (you and me) become more like the master (our Lord). This is a more worthy goal than the one implicit in the Kingsbury list, but still . . . I sometimes wonder if there is something missing.

The question at the root of every book, manual, curriculum, or program that is sold is this: How do we change? How do we make our life decision stick to our life as we live it? Can each of us actually become the kind of person we read about in our devotional books? We can surely study more; we can easily talk less. We would all do well to listen to wisdom from our elders and from the biblical record. But seldom do these efforts produce any change at all. Who we are appears to be hard-wired in us. Our nature—its strengths, weaknesses, proclivities, and values—appears, for all intents and purposes, to be baked in the cake.

But the Bible shows us a new way to change. To put it in the language of the self-help industry, there is a better, faster, and permanent way to achieve "breakthrough results."

The way the student becomes like the master is not just by learning from the master thought by thought, point by point, or even verse by verse. This method is important, but it is not the only way, and it may not even be the best way. To become like the master, the student must actually *do* what the master has done. To become like the Lord in ways that we would want, we can learn from him not only word by word, but also by walking with him, step-by-step: to do what he did; to love the way he loved; to go where he went; to act as he would act.

In other words, when Jesus says, "Follow me," he is not inviting us only to come and see, but also to come and learn, and then go and do.

James, John, and Who's on First

Matthew recorded an interesting anecdote in the twentieth chapter of his gospel. The situation is this: Jesus has just finished one of his most perplexing teachings, the parable of the workers in the vineyard. In the story, Jesus relates a payroll principle that you won't learn in the course of your Harvard

MBA. He tells of a landowner who goes down to the local market square to hire day laborers, much as people now go to the unemployment office to find workers willing to do odd jobs for a day's wage. The landowner arrives early in the day, as one would expect, and agrees with several people to pay them a standard amount for a day of work.

A little later, he goes in search of some more workers. He makes the same agreement with them, and they come to work for him, also. He makes three more trips to the unemployment office: at midday, in midafternoon, and at about five o'clock, offering the same terms each time. At the end of the day, he instructs his accountant to pay each of the laborers the same amount of money—even the ones who had only been working for an hour.

If you were one of the guys who had been working since just after sunup and you got paid the same as somebody who didn't show up until five o'clock, would you have any questions for the boss? The workers in Jesus' parable certainly did. "These last worked only one hour, and you have made them equal to us who have borne the burden of the day and the scorching heat" (Matthew 20:12).

Did the landowner smack his forehead, grimace, apologize, and boost the pay of those who had worked more hours? No. Here's what he said: "Friend, I am doing you no wrong. Did you not agree with me for a denarius? Take what belongs to you and go. I choose to give to this last worker as I give to you. Am I not allowed to do what I choose with what belongs to me? Or do you begrudge my generosity?" (vv. 13–15).

And then, Jesus delivers the punch line: "So the last will be first, and the first last" (v. 16).

How's that for an HR policy? The landowner paid each worker exactly what the worker agreed to, as he asserted. The problem, as far as the early birds were concerned, was that he decided to be more liberal with the payroll than was customary or expected. He wanted, because of his generosity, to give those who came last the very same benefit as those who came first. The economy of the kingdom of heaven, *You are valued because you were called, not because of how you performed.* in other words, does not run according to the same rules as the economy of the kingdoms of this world. God's organizational chart, as with Mrs. Turpin's vision in Flannery O'Connor's classic story, "Revelation," puts the "bottom rail on top."

The parable gives specific instruction for all Christians. It tells believers that they are to live within a new economic model. Labor is always going to be exchanged for money. That is the way of the world. And thus it will ever be. But in the new economy, as shown in the parable, no one is ever worth less than anyone else. You are valued because you were called, not because of how you performed, how long you have worked, or what you have produced. The generous heart of the employer overwhelms everyone in the parable. And it says to us: go and do likewise; overwhelm everyone you can with a love and affection that isn't tied to their performance but to their covenant with our generous God.

Having concluded that surprising bit of instruction, Jesus next tells his followers, as they journey toward Jerusalem, that he is going to be delivered up to death, but that he will be resurrected on the third day. The Master is knowingly and voluntarily surrendering himself to the indignities that will be heaped on him by his enemies . . . but the result will be his ultimate victory. Once again, the One who is first places himself last, and by doing so assures his ultimate preeminence.

Scripture does not record the disciples' immediate reaction to this pronouncement of Jesus. However, we may suppose that many of its implications did not sink in, because of what happened next.

The mother of James and John, whom Jesus nicknamed "the sons of thunder," came to Jesus with a request that any mom, anywhere in the world, would surely understand: "Say that these two sons of mine are to sit, one at your right hand and one at your left, in your kingdom" (Matthew 20:21). Mrs. Zebedee wanted Jesus to do right by her boys! She wanted James and John to have the inside track.

I can almost imagine Jesus giving her a sad smile as he looked first at the mother, then at her sons. "Jesus answered, 'You do not know what you are asking. Are you able to drink the cup that I am to drink?'" (v. 22). Remember: he has just told them that he is going to Jerusalem to be crucified. Is this really the time to be angling for promotions?

Of course, the other ten disciples caught wind of what was going on, and they became incensed at the thought of James and John trying to pull off such a coup. So, Jesus called a group meeting to explain to everyone—yet another time—that in the corporation he was founding, the usual rules of hierarchy did not apply:

> You know that the rulers of the Gentiles lord it over them, and their great ones exercise authority over them. It shall not be so among you. But whoever would be great among you must be your servant, and whoever would be first among you must be your slave, even as the Son of Man came not to be served but to serve, and to give his life as a ransom for many. (Matthew 20:25–28)

"Who wants to be first?" Jesus asks. "That person needs to put himself or herself last. In my outfit, the commanding officer carries the buck private's gear. In my banquet hall, the master washes the guests' feet."

Giving up . . . letting go of our privileges . . . releasing our selfish expectations . . . This is the disciple's way.

The "Halo Effect"

So how do we get there? How do we internalize the counter-cultural way of life exemplified by Jesus, Paul, and other great believers throughout history?

I'm afraid it won't happen simply by willpower, nor is a list of "thou shalt nots" likely to inspire us to authentic ser-vanthood. Instead, we must substitute the positive value of generosity for the negative pressure of the tyranny of self.

The great theologian and philosopher Thomas Aquinas knew this back in the thirteenth century. His magnum opus, *Summa Theologiae*, lays out the ways he believed that the best path to goodness in humanity is the positive encouragement of virtue, rather than suppression of the negative energies of vice. He said, "Good can exist without evil, whereas evil cannot exist without good." During Aquinas's time, the concept of "cardinal virtues," as opposed to "cardinal vices," gained great influence in the church. Sometimes, the virtues were called "contrary virtues," because they were said to oppose the vices, countering the temptation to succumb to them. The virtue of generosity, in this way of thinking, counters the temptation to greed; it substitutes a positive good for a negative prohibition.

But long before Aquinas, Jesus taught his followers that, rather than trying to go out and pull up all the weeds in the field, they should simply let the crops grow. At the end, during the harvest, the Master Farmer will be able to separate what is good from what is bad (Matthew 13:24–29). And isn't this same principle borne out every spring in countless lawns across our land? In the southern part of the country, where I live, the two favorite yard grasses—Bermuda grass and St. Augustine grass—are famous for their ability to cover an area of ground when soil and sunlight conditions are right. Weeds may temporarily sprout during the early spring, but by the time summer gets rolling, the vigorously growing grass will choke them out, spreading a carpet of green turf where the unruly "tares" once sprouted.

We can go back much further in time, to that wild mountaintop in the Sinai wilderness where God gave Moses the Ten Commandments. Consider the order in which the Decalogue is presented (Exodus 20:1–17):

1. Worship only God.

2. Don't worship idols.

3. Use God's name properly.

4. Respect the holiness of the Sabbath.

5. Honor your parents.

6. Do not murder.

7. Do not commit adultery.

8. Do not steal.

9. Do not give false testimony.

10. Do not covet.

God's legal code for his chosen people starts in the most positive place of all: the character of God himself. He announced that he, and he only, is the proper object of reverence and worship: "I am the LORD your God, who brought you out of the land of Egypt, out of the house of slavery" (Exodus 20:2). God founds everything that follows on his gracious deliverance of his people. Because he is the one who freed them, he is the only one they are to worship.

At the end of the list is "Do not covet." Thus God places the vice of greed at the bottom, only after providing to Israel all the other positive attributes that he wished them to exemplify.

But do you notice that the very last commandment is really the most difficult one to keep? Think about it. I know what it means to "Do no murder": so far, so good—I have not murdered. I can always know what it means NOT to murder. And I know what it means not to commit adultery in my marriage to Fran; that is an act of will that, so far, I'm okay on. Mission accomplished! But the lower on the list I get, the harder and harder it is for me to actually do or achieve. I do not steal as a matter of habit. But honestly, I have found myself "borrowing indefinitely" things that don't belong to me. (I have a nice collection of umbrellas that were "left for lost" at the church!) I find it all but impossible never to lie or spread a false rumor. I sometimes traffic in "fake news" . . . and like to!

But the last command is totally impossible to keep! No coveting? No coveting my neighbor's possessions? His life? His wife? His car? What about his chain saw? Or his low mortgage interest rate?

Coveting is the hallmark of the American way of life, isn't it? I cloak the term "covet" in words such as "admire" or "be impressed with" or even "stare," but it is impossible to look at my neighbor's new truck or grill or lawn or job or recent vacation without "coveting": hoping that I could one day have something like that myself. Greed is ubiquitous. And in my view, it is impossible to eliminate it simply by its prohibition as a commandment. Just as Paul noted in Romans 7:7, we "would not have known what it is to covet if the law had not said, 'You shall not covet.'" It's like someone today saying to us,

"Whatever you do, don't think about a pink elephant." When you hear that, what is the first image that pops into your mind? Me too!

But if I cannot uproot it . . . I can displace it. Why? Because if greed exists in the mind and the heart, it can be displaced by its positive counterpart, generosity. Indeed, as we will see, greed, or covetousness, is a vice, and generosity is the only way to displace it. The benefit of a virtue is that once it takes up residence in the human consciousness, it begins to effect change. It rearranges the furniture of our mental and emotional dwelling, and by the time it has finished its redecorating project, there is no room left for greed and covetousness.

Some time ago, I came across a remarkable piece of wisdom, penned by a Scottish pastor toward the middle of the nineteenth century. In his tract, *The Expulsive Power of a New Affection*, Thomas Chalmers wrote:

There are two ways in which a practical moralist may attempt to displace from the human heart its love of the world—either by a demonstration of the world's vanity, so as that the heart shall be prevailed upon simply to withdraw its regard from an object that is not worthy of it; or, by setting forth another object, even God, as more worthy of its attachment, so as that the heart shall be prevailed upon not to resign an old affection, which shall have nothing to succeed it, but to exchange an old affection for a new one.

My purpose is to show, that from the constitution of our nature, the former method is altogether incompetent and ineffectual and that the latter method will alone suffice for the rescue and recovery of the heart from the wrong affection that domineers over it.[2]

Modern researchers might know this as a "halo effect." The term is nearly one hundred years old, but its reference is universal and timeless. It refers to the tendency of one action or attitude to impact a second or third action or attitude in a like way. Once one thing is settled, its impact will continue to have sway.

Indeed, notice the title of the essay. The word used is *Expulsive*, concerning a person's conversion experience. I am sure we all would love to see the word *Explosive*, as if somehow the mere act of repentance would be enough to kill all sin and guilt. But what Chalmers knew—along with Aquinas, Paul, and Christ—is that the only way to overcome the basic selfishness of the human heart, in this age or any other, is to displace it with the regenerative, Godlike quality of generosity. If we can learn to give up, we can change our world.

---

[2] Thomas Chalmers, *The Expulsive Power of a New Affection* (Edinburgh: Thomas Constable, 1855; repr. Curiosmith, 2012), 7.

KEY POINTS

- Despite our fascination with self-improvement, we are not actually effective at changing our behaviors.

- The church has focused most of its discipleship programming on learning (reading, viewing, and discussing) curriculum.

- Transformative discipleship occurs as disciples follow and imitate their master.

- When we follow Jesus, we are invited into a radically generous way of living in the world.

- The virtue of generosity and focus on others is the only antidote to the vice of greed and selfishness that seems so inescapable.

QUESTIONS FOR DISCUSSION

1. Debate the following statement: Bible studies and other Christian education courses will not be enough to form disciples of Christ.

2. Recall an experience in which you were able to alter habits and attitudes you had held for a long time. What was able to create that sort of change?

3. Talk about some of the challenges Jesus gave his disciples in order to follow him. Were those challenges more about adopting ideas and beliefs or about practices and actions?

4. Do you think you can stop being selfish? What would it take to make that happen?

CHAPTER 6

MIRACLE IN MACEDONIA: A CASE STUDY

———•———

One in Christ?

The church arose in a Jewish context; after all, its Lord was born into a Jewish home, the son of a Jewish mother, a descendant of the royal line of David. He came as the Messiah promised by repeated prophecy throughout the history of the Jewish people, beginning with God's promise to Abraham at the very establishment of the Jewish nation: "I will make of you a great nation, and I will bless you and make your name great, so that you will be a blessing. I will bless those who bless you, and him who dishonors you I will curse, *and in you all the families of the earth shall be blessed*" (Genesis 12:2–3; emphasis added).

All of Jesus' original disciples were Jews. His earliest apostles were Jews. As far as we can determine from the biblical record, every single person who heard Peter's sermon on the day of Pentecost, when the church was born, was Jewish; they were in Jerusalem to celebrate the Feast of Tabernacles—a Jewish holiday!

But God had plans for this new fellowship that went far beyond the biological descendants of Abraham. God's plans encompassed every man, woman, and child in the whole world, from every tribe and nation. As he said in his calling of Abraham, "all the families of the earth" would be blessed. Through the prophet Isaiah, God says to his people, "It is too light a thing that you should be my servant to raise up the tribes of Jacob and to bring back the preserved of Israel; I will make you as a light for the nations [the Gentiles], that my salvation may reach to the end of the earth" (Isaiah 49:6).

Thus, God sent a message to Peter in the person of Cornelius, a devout man who was not a Jew. By means of an unforgettable vision, followed by some pretty unmistakable signs, God let Peter know for certain that the message of the risen Christ was to be shared with all people, everywhere—not just Jews.

But there was a problem. For centuries, faithful Jews had believed that God's law prohibited them from having close fellowship with uncircumcised "Gentiles": people from non-Jewish nations who did not follow the rules of God's ancient covenant with Abraham. How was this new church thing going to work? How were Jews and non-Jews supposed to cooperate in spreading the good news? What, in fact, was the good news?

It was a serious and fundamental problem for the infant church. And it began to manifest almost immediately. In Acts 6, we read of a problem that occurred in Jerusalem, in the earliest days, when many people from far provinces of the Roman Empire who had come for that original Feast of Tabernacles were still in the Holy City. Many people were coming to belief in the Messiah and were staying in Jerusalem, not wanting to leave this amazing, new community that was forming. And so, as we know from Acts 4, many of the believers were liquidating their holdings in order to provide for those separated from their usual means of support.

But there was a problem: the widows—already dependent on others for support in this patriarchal society—were not being treated equally in the distribution of food. Those from Jerusalem and the surrounding area—who presumably had close kinship ties with many in Jerusalem—were being better cared for than the widows from farther away, in the Greek-speaking parts of the Roman Empire. As a result, the apostles appointed the first deacons to oversee the fairness of the food distribution.

If the church had a problem with preferential treatment between Greek-speaking and non-Greek-speaking Jewish widows, what in the world would happen when people came into the fellowship who weren't even Jewish? Surely such a divide would be too great for humans to overcome. How would it be possible to maintain the unity of Christ among people who had so little in common?

Peter's vision and his experience with Cornelius, recorded in Acts 10, was proof positive that God intended for the chasm between Jew and Gentile to be bridged. When Peter told Cornelius and his servants the story of Jesus, God's Holy Spirit fell on these non-Jewish believers, in the same way as he had come upon Peter and the other apostles on the day of Pentecost. Peter said, "Can anyone withhold water for baptizing these people, who have received the Holy Spirit just as we have?" (v. 47).

Soon after, God commissioned Paul to preach the gospel of Christ among the Gentiles. He literally knocked this violent persecutor of Christians off his horse, on the way to Damascus, to convince him that he should take the good news to people everywhere. The mission to the Gentiles was truly under way.

But problems remained. We read in Acts 15, "Some men came down from Judea and were teaching the brothers: 'Unless you are circumcised, according to the custom of Moses, you cannot be saved'" (v. 1). These people from Jerusalem just could not believe that God really meant to do away with the covenant of circumcision given to Abraham. They meant to see that these new Gentile believers got the message.

But Paul and Barnabas, who had witnessed God working mightily among non-Jews throughout the Mediterranean basin, would have none of it. They engaged in sharp dispute with the people from Jerusalem. As a result, they were dispatched to Jerusalem—at that time, still the center of the church and the home of most of its leadership—to meet with the other apostles and leaders about this very crucial question. The outcome of the meeting was a rather modest list of tenets to which the leaders asked the non-Jewish Christians to subscribe: a few dietary restrictions out of deference for Jews, and sexual purity.

As a result, when the letter containing these directives was read by the non-Jewish Christians up in Antioch, they "rejoiced because of its encouragement" (Acts 15:31). In other words, they did not have to become culturally Jewish to remain in saving fellowship with Christ. As a result of this first church council, the gospel was poised to spread throughout the Roman world, as it soon did—in large part, due to the efforts of Paul.

Hard Times in Judea

But more trouble was coming from a different quarter. Agabus, a Christian from Jerusalem with the gift of prophecy, journeyed north to Antioch with some sobering news. At the end of Acts 11, we read that he stood up in the assembly of the church in Antioch and, under the direct influence of the Holy Spirit, announced that a widespread famine was coming. (Luke, the writer of Acts, helpfully noted that this famine actually occurred during the reign of Claudius Caesar, who ruled from AD 41 to 54.)

The response of the non-Jewish Christians to this announcement was remarkable: they resolved to give money to aid the impoverished Christians in Judea—the homeland of the Jews. Luke simply records, "The disciples determined, every one according to his ability, to send relief to the brothers living in Judea. And they did so, sending it to the elders by the hand of Barnabas and Saul" (Acts 11:29–30).

Such a short notice, but such an astounding undertaking! In fact, Paul would devote significant time in his missionary journeys to taking up this collection—gathered primarily from Gentiles—that would directly benefit the Jewish Christians of Judea.

Can you imagine the impact this gift must have had on the Jewish believers? Sorely needed resources were provided to them, and it came from people they had never seen and were likely never to meet! Not only that, but their benefactors did not even share their Jewish heritage. The only link between them, actually, was the family link provided by the blood of Jesus: they were, as Acts 11:29 says, "brothers and sisters" in Christ (NIV). Could there have been any more powerful way to graphically enact the unity of the body of Christ than to have one group caring so generously for another, even though the two were culturally and geographically divided?

Bridging the Impossible

The gift of the Gentile believers for the relief of the beleaguered Judean Christians provided a bridge across a chasm that could never have been spanned by merely human means. The virtue of generosity forged a bond between two groups—Jews and Gentiles—that were previously considered inherently incompatible. In the process, the earliest Christians realized that what united them was far greater than what divided them. They experienced firsthand the new family that God was forging. Their common bloodline didn't depend on family trees but on the uniting, cleansing blood of Christ.

The testimony of generosity was powerful in the first century, and it is no less so today. A friend told me recently about the honor of witnessing the baptism of a young man from a fundamentalist Muslim country. When explaining what led him to

Christ, the young convert said, "These Christians were kind to me; they opened their homes to me. They were generous." This young seeker was captivated by the love of those who took Jesus at his word when he said, "It is more blessed to give than to receive."

The body of Christ is at its best and most powerful when it is at its most giving. Paul knew that, and he took the message everywhere. We need to hear the same message today, with new ears, refreshed hearts, heightened faith, and deep urgency. A hurting world depends on us.

Do you see the common thread here? People were giving up to God all over the place. The hard-liners in Jerusalem were giving up their old traditions to welcome in the newest converts in Asia. The converts in Asia were giving up their money and resources to underwrite and support people who used to hate them. Paul was giving up his time and energy to collect money he himself would never see. The first Christians were giving up their prerogatives to call the shots on who was the best, first, and highest class of gender, ethnicity, and life status. The impression you have when reading the letters of Paul is that people were giving up to God everything that had formerly described their life; even to their own identity!

The body of Christ is at its best and most powerful when it is at its most giving.

In this way, read the words of the apostle Paul in Colossians 3 as if for the first time. Count the number of things, attitudes, behaviors, prerogatives, and resources Paul was calling upon his readers to "give up"!

KEY POINTS

- Generosity was an important key to unity and cohesiveness in the early church.

- Generosity helped bridge the divide between Jewish and non-Jewish believers.

- Paul correlated the generosity of the Macedonian believers with their faith and commended them as examples to others.

- Paul encouraged generosity as a key value for followers of Jesus.

- Generosity offers a powerful testimony to the non-Christian world.

QUESTIONS FOR DISCUSSION

1. What do you think causes most "church fights"? Specifically, what are the postures and attitudes that lead to division within the church?

2. How might a renewed focus on generosity work to create an atmosphere that could weather conflict or uncertainty?

3. Have you ever witnessed a division that was healed through generosity? How did it happen?

4. Can you think of a problem facing your local church or the broader fellowship that might be solved or eased by generosity? How would this look, if it were to happen?

5. What gives the testimony of generosity its power? Why do you think it works as it does?

CHAPTER 7

Helping the Church Give Up

———•———

It's all well and good to talk about giving up in the life of Jesus and Paul and the early church, but how do we recover—after all these intervening centuries—that laser focus on generosity? There isn't a simple answer. But when we look at the state of giving today and when we notice all the destructive ways the church has spoken about giving, we see the urgent need to come up with a new game plan for establishing generosity.

The State of Generosity

For decades in the United States, religious giving has reliably been the largest single segment of the charitable donation ecosystem. This continued to be true in 2014, according to the annual report from the Giving USA Foundation, a Chicago-based not-for-profit. But for a number of years, religious giving has been slowing, a trend that continued in 2014, according to the study. After adjustment for inflation, giving to religious organizations grew at less than 1 percent, year over year: the smallest increase among all categories of giving. While religious giving remains the largest single sector—for now—it is rapidly losing ground, falling from 53 percent of all donations in 1987 to just 32 percent in 2014.[1]

What if we read the last paragraph and instead of giving, we substituted the word *discipleship* or *worship attendance* or *missionary support*? There would be think-tank discussions and conferences on the subject. Christians would be talking about it more and more. Seminaries would be training young leaders to address the "growing crisis in discipleship that is being forecast in our church." I am simply suggesting here that we notice the problem. Religious giving, acts of generosity, are weakening in our churches.

Now, in all fairness, we should realize that the news on Christian giving is not all bad. For example, as just noted, religious giving, despite being in a slide, still accounts for the largest single segment of charitable donations in this country. And in many surveys, the total charitable giving of Christians—including not just what they put in the collection plate at church, but also the money, time, and property they donate to other charitable efforts—compares very favorably to the nonreligious population. In their 2008 book *Passing the Plate: Why American Christians Don't Give Away More Money*, Christian Smith, Michael O. Emerson, and Patricia Snell noted that 50 percent of nonreligious Americans give

---

[1] Schuyler Velasco, "Charitable Giving Sets New Record, but Why Are Religious Donations Waning?" *Christian Science Monitor*, June 16, 2015, http://www.csmonitor.com/Business/2015/0616/Charitable-giving-sets-new-record-but-why-are-religious-donations-waning.

nothing at all to charity,[2] while, according to a study released in November 2013, 65 percent of Americans who claim a religious affiliation make some amount of voluntary, charitable gifts.[3] Further, Smith, Emerson, and Snell assert that, while the average American Christian gives nearly 3 percent of total income to charity, nonbelievers give, on the average, less than 1 percent. So, the giving landscape, from a Christian perspective, is not entirely bleak.

But, oh, my goodness, we should be doing so much more! As the authors of *Passing the Plate* also stated, American Christians—"the most affluent single group of Christians in two thousand years of church history"—are, in terms of capability to give, penurious to the point of disobedience! According to the authors, at least 20 percent of self-identified American Christians give nothing at all![4]

What Happened?

What are the factors that have caused the church, famous in its infancy and youth as a community of selfless givers, to move into the position it occupies today in the minds of much of the unchurched world? How did we go from a

---

[2] Christian Smith, Michael O. Emerson, and Patricia Snell, *Passing the Plate: Why American Christians Don't Give Away More Money* (New York: Oxford University Press, 2008), 29.

[3] Alex Daniels, "Religious Americans Give More, New Study Finds." *Chronicle of Philanthropy*, November 25, 2013, https://www.philanthropy.com/article/Religious-Americans-Give-More/153973.

[4] Smith, Emerson, and Snell, *Passing the Plate*, 3.

situation where, in AD 197, Tertullian could write of Christians' well-known self-sacrificial behavior with no fear of being contradicted, to today, when Christians are roundly—and too often, justly—accused of all sorts of mean-spirited behavior, including selfishness?

Part of the answer may lie in the way so many of the church's ministry functions became institutionalized over the centuries. In the earliest days, giving was deeply personal: the Jewish Christians in Jerusalem willingly and lovingly placed their resources in the hands of Stephen and his fellow deacons; the Greek-speaking widows who received these life-sustaining distributions were able to connect a face and a giving heart to the gift. Later, when Paul made his collection in Macedonia, he specifically noted the personal nature of the gifts and the motivation for them: "They gave themselves first to the Lord" (2 Corinthians 8:5). As we have seen, during the horrendous plagues of the second and third centuries, Christians went to their neighbors, both pagan and Christian, to offer help, putting their own lives at risk in the process. In all of these instances, the giving was intimately connected to the person offering and the person receiving it.

As time went on, this same impulse to generosity and caring for the helpless motivated the establishment of countless hospitals, orphanages, and shelters for the poor and indigent. The church, motivated by the One who said, "It is better to give than to receive," was the first entity in the history of the Western world to undertake the wide-scale establishment of places specifically devoted to the care of the sick, the weak, the young, and the infirm.

But this work, as good and necessary as it was, may have come at an unexpected price. By beginning to relocate the responsibility of caring for others from each individual Christian to institutions overseen by a professional clerical/medical class, the church may also have initiated a process that separated individual Christians from feeling the responsibility of caring for those in need. Over time, this process likely crystallized to a certain extent, such that it eventually became "their" responsibility—the clergy and others in positions of "official" leadership—to see to the needs of the disadvantaged. In other words, when the church obscures the connection between the giver and the one who receives, it may also unwittingly undermine a central motivation for individual Christians to give.

What about the Prosperity Gospel?

As the secular, selfie-based culture has gained more and more traction, personal giving has been on the decline. It is not hard to see why. My Best Buy moment (see chapter 1) is a perfect example of the large issues. Selfie theology is, after all, all about the self. Giving sacrificially, certainly to an institution, doesn't fit with the way we've been wired to think.

But what if there was a message about stewardship, generosity, and giving that, rather than challenging the selfie theology of the current times, actually embraced it? What if there was a way to take the message of giving up to God and merge it with our innate desire to have a great life? With this one simple, emphatic message, giving could increase *and* my living could expand. Giving up could allow me to live it up. That would be a win-win!

Creating a win-win is the essential message of the "prosperity gospel" and it has taken hold of large sections of the Christian church in the West and overseas. It is based on a very selfie-focused metaphor. The thought process goes something like this: *My Father in heaven is rich beyond my dreams. He is a King of a kingdom and owns the cattle on a thousand hills. I am a King's child, and I have the right of living like my Father wants. My Father King would never want me to be poor . . . so I conclude that he wants me to be blessed, to be wealthy. If I live out the tenets of the New Testament teaching on money, God will prosper me. In fact, he is just waiting for me to ask and show how serious I am. He is waiting for me to give a financial seed gift, a kick-starter amount of money. In short, if I want to live it up, I have to give it up! If I prime the pump, the Lord will open the floodgates!*

But wait! There's more!

Are you successful, healthy, wealthy, and generally pleased with your lot in life? Congratulations! You are, by definition, living in the center of God's will! Do you want to get even bigger blessings? Great! All you need to do is contribute more and God will reciprocate by pouring abundance into your lap. Giving isn't really giving; it's an investment. And, they say, God's ROI (return on investment) is off the charts. After all, isn't this what Jesus promises in Luke 6:38, when he says, "Give, and it will be given to you . . ."?

And to further prove the point as well as confuse the issue, we can all share stories about God's provision in our lives, our experience of plenty, and the prosperity we have enjoyed. There are times when Fran and I have given generously and we have also received generously. It is hard not to make the one-to-one connection. Indeed, if I collected stories and testimonies of how God seemingly blessed others who gave sacrificially to the work of the church, I'd have enough to fill a large book of verified stories from real-life people.

But this sounds too good to be true! And it is. It is a false gospel because it is no gospel at all. There is nothing Christian or cross-centered about it. But like all heresies, it contains just enough truth to make it attractive, if not plausible.

In fact, we are wrong in our thinking if we believe that the God of the Bible is just waiting to shower us with blessing tomorrow if we prime the pump today. That is a kind of control of God's hand that simply does not square with the teaching of the Old and New Testaments. Actually, that is how magic works: you say the right formula and—*poof!*—you get the wished-for result. In some places, the belief that you can do something here on earth to cause some supernatural outcome to occur is called voodoo.

Sadly, by wrenching Bible verses out of context and repackaging them for maximum marketing appeal, apostles of the prosperity gospel have led thousands astray, teaching them to see God as some kind of divine deal maker, ruled by the principle of *quid pro quo*. Like the ancient pagan deities, the god of the prosperity gospel responds to those who make the appropriate offering. The prosperity gospel is, at its root, no more or less than idolatry dressed up in church clothes. It is the golden calf, sitting at the front of the church sanctuary. If I bow to it, maybe it will bend toward me.

The prosperity gospel is, as Shakespeare wrote, "the seeming truth which cunning times put on to entrap the wisest."[5] It is, we might say, nearly true, and certainly so for the upwardly mobile religious crowd at whom it is aimed. But around the world, in shantytowns and in rural African churches, in the old steel mill towns along the Allegheny River or the persecuted churches in Arab countries, the rule of "give it up so you can live it up" cannot apply. Some brothers in Sudan live on less than $250 a year. That is not enough to prime any pump.

So here is a mystery I must simply put forth: While I have seen this blessing and provision happen in my life too often to be coincidental, *receiving them can never be the motivation for giving.* Whatever blessings come by way of giving, if they become the *main focus* for our giving, we have entered into error. Indeed, the central fallacy of the prosperity gospel can also be its main attraction. It teaches that not only can you have the wealth, influence, and blessing you seek, but also that receiving all this is actually what God desires for you.

If receiving becomes the main focus for our giving, we have entered into error.

---

[5] William Shakespeare, *The Merchant of Venice*, act 3, sc. 2, ln. 102.

It seems to me that Christians can trust the words of the Lord Jesus, who said, "It is more blessed to give than to receive" (Acts 20:35). Modern motivational preachers might have said it backwards, "It is a blessing to receive, so give!" That is indeed backwards. But Jesus put the emphasis on the giving; he put whatever might come back as "reward" in second place. Once again, Jesus' unwritten teaching on the subject strikes the perfect chord. It is all about generosity. It is about being generous (freely giving), not seeming to be generous (expecting something in return).

Recovering the Generosity Gene

Since it was first published in 1862, Victor Hugo's immortal story *Les Misérables* has captured the hearts and imaginations of untold thousands. Most recently, this tale of the power of forgiveness and sacrifice has swept away theater audiences, first with the Tony Award–winning musical adaptation and then with the movie treatment, which garnered an Academy Award for Best Supporting Actress for Anne Hathaway. In fact, Hugo's story has been adapted for mass media a total of nine times, beginning with a 1935 movie that was nominated for three trophies at the Eighth Academy Awards.

Who doesn't know the dramatic turning point of the story? Jean Valjean, only recently released from prison, is caught red-handed leaving town with silverware belonging to Bishop Myriel of Digne, who gave the ex-convict shelter when no one else would. Hauled by the police back to the bishop's home, Valjean listens, dumbstruck, as the bishop assures the arresting officers that the silverware has not been stolen; he has given it to Valjean as a gift to help him on his way. "Well, but how is this?" he says, "I gave you the candlesticks too, which are of silver like the rest, and for which you can certainly get two hundred francs. Why did you not carry them away with your forks and spoons?" As the bishop hands the candlesticks to the ex-convict, the officers leave, and the bishop says to the astounded Valjean, "My brother, you no longer belong to evil, but to good. It is your soul that I buy from you; I withdraw it from black thoughts and the spirit of perdition, and I give it to God."[6] This hardened man, with all the human tenderness and trust hammered out of him by years of cruel imprisonment, was changed in an instant by a single act of generosity and grace.

Why has Hugo's tale stood the test of time, continuing to transport audiences even in our cynical, self-absorbed age? I believe it is because of the power of generosity and our instinctive need to believe that such generosity is possible. Something in each of us yearns to hear the same words that the bishop pronounces over Valjean: "You no longer belong to evil, but to good . . . Your soul belongs to God."

By now, I hope it seems clear to you that the way for the people of Christ to win the hearts and minds of a selfish, dying world is to discover the power, joy, and fulfillment that comes from giving up—from offering ourselves and our

---

[6] Victor Hugo, Les Misérables, chap. 12, http://www.online-literature.com /victor_hugo/les_miserables/26/, accessed May 13, 2017.

resources in generous service to others in the name of Christ. Not only is the world waiting to hear this message, though; Christ's church is waiting to be sent on this mission!

So how can church leaders begin to create a culture of giving up? As I said, there's not going to be a simple answer to this. Every church has to understand the context in which it operates and discern the best way to start these conversations. In the final chapter, we'll discuss some big ideas that can begin to nudge churches back toward a heart of generosity.

 KEY POINTS

- The church is still generous compared to secular culture, but religious giving is declining at an alarming rate.

- The prosperity gospel warps the truth of God's abundant blessing by attaching it to the prevailing narrative of consumerism.

- Giving in the model of the prosperity gospel is plain idolatry.

- In the face of such idolatry, unexpected and radical generosity kindles faith in those who see and receive it.

DISCUSSION QUESTIONS

1. Why do you think giving is on the decline in American churches over the last several decades? Try to rank the contributing factors.

2. What is the appeal of the prosperity gospel?

3. Why is it difficult to see through the falsehood of this message?

4. Is there a practical way to give the way Jesus gave? What would that look like as a practice in your church?

CHAPTER 8

TEN BIG IDEAS FOR THE GENEROUS CHURCH

———•———

Remember: Building a culture of generosity is not primarily a budget enhancement program to get more money for the church. It is not just another missions or outreach program with extra resources of time and money to give away. Focusing on the value of generosity in the life of the church will increase generosity "*for* the pews," so to speak. But it will also empower ministry "*from* the pews." Both will happen.

But it needs to be emphasized once again: the real purpose of creating a culture of generosity is to help each member live more and more as Jesus lived. *Esse Quam Videri.* A culture of generosity helps the church better live out its call to be a witness to Christ in an unbelieving world. Because his life was all about "giving up," so should our lives be as well.

Christ Church, where I pastored for so many years, was the laboratory for many of the suggestions I offer to you in this final chapter. It was a joy and a privilege to lead this great church through three decades of effort to become a generous church in our community, our membership, the mission field, and the denomination of which we are a part. The staff and leadership who served alongside me were more than flexible and even more generous with their own time and commitment to our mission. Many of the ideas that follow were hard-wired into the church in the early days. Every year, as we tried new ways of teaching old truths, I knew that I was depending on the credibility of my leadership and my longevity. Every church is different, and every church leader will need to find ways to adopt or adapt these ideas (and others) into the common life of the church. An older, seasoned church might find some of these ideas too startling. In fact, some of these plans were scuttled before they were attempted because of staff concerns about their propriety. Others may find them way too tame. But they were as far as I could see to take the church in the area of generosity.

Here, then, are some of the key features of the generous church. If you and your church want to grow in this area, I would invite you to consider these ideas.

1. Name It!

Yes, the first step to developing a culture of generosity in the local church is to name the value of generosity and claim it as a goal. Simply stated, the first step toward connecting with the transformational power of generosity is to start talking about it. Pray about it. Discuss it. Preach about it. Teach about it. Use the word routinely. The leaders of a congregation could write about generosity in bulletins, blurbs, and announcements. It is one of the few unbreakable truths of church life: you get more of whatever you pay attention to. Stop paying attention to what people are not doing (not giving) and instead pay attention to what your members are all called to do (be givers!).

I think that sometimes we as Christians—and especially pastors—try to be so careful to avoid "guilting" people over their giving that we just never get around to mentioning it at all. This topic, which was so central to the life of the early church, receives dreadfully short shrift in our congregations today. I know of pastors who, with visible reluctance, will hold up a pledge card when budget time rolls around each year, telling their congregations to "think about it," or something equally vague, and leave it at that. No wonder we have such a standoffish attitude toward generosity! We treat it like some kind of social disease that should only be mentioned when there is no other choice!

I'm reminded here of Pastor Rick Warren's distaste for false modesty as just another form of self-centeredness. He said, "Humility is not thinking less of yourself; it's thinking of yourself less."[1] As a church leader, if you are self-conscious when talking about money, it just draws attention to you—it makes people think that giving always comes back to you. Get over it! Talk about money with the confident knowledge that what is given goes toward expanding the kingdom. Your example will help others learn to stop being embarrassed about their giving and begin to encourage others.

---

[1] Rick Warren, *The Purpose Driven Life: What on Earth Am I Here For?* (Grand Rapids: Zondervan, 2002), day 19.

Other pastors and leaders are concerned that too much talk about money will drive people away. Well, that might be true. *But we cannot let the least committed in the church set the agenda for the rest.* If some people have money issues with the church, the pastor can defuse that bomb by exposing it. Say, for example, the pastor plans a sermon series on generosity. The preacher can simply say something like this: "Some of you have real questions about how the church raises and accounts for its money. I want to be totally transparent about what we think about money, how we raise it, where it comes from, and how it is accounted for. You will learn a lot about the values of our church in the next few weeks as I preach on this subject. So, stay around. In fact, most people attending a church want to know how the church raises, uses, accounts for, and gives away its money."

And the opposite is true for seasoned givers. People who have given in the past know the strong sense of joy and thanksgiving with which they gave. And generally, they love to talk about how giving has affected their lives. I have not ever known any giver to brag about his or her giving, but all generous givers have something in common: they have experienced a sense of infectious joy. They love to hear about the joy that others have received.

Personally, I tried never to shy away from talking about this fascinating subject. In fact, I have seen it as an automatic way to gain someone's attention. Here is my reasoning: we have so little in common with everyone else. Our lives, our ages and stages, are often vastly different from each other's.

A shopkeeper has a different life than a shipyard worker; a nurse spends her days differently than a lawyer. What do we have in common, really?

Actually, there are a few things everyone has in common; only three things that we share with others as a matter of fact. Only three. Each person on the planet, as long as he or she is alive, has three things in common with everyone else: (1) the relentless passage of time; (2) the work and effort we spend to do something with that time; and (3) the collection, use, disbursement, and stewardship of resources. That is it! Time, talent, and our use of treasure are the most common denominators for everyone on the planet. Put another way, time, talent, and treasure are the universal currency of the living. And that makes any conversation about them a fascinatingly personal event.

2. Generously Preach Generosity

Getting things out in the open has to start from the pulpit. It's admirable that some pastors carve out time every year to preach on giving, but too often I've heard sermons that sounded apologetic and defensive. Pastors and preachers be advised: you aren't coming to your congregation with your hat in hand. Instead, you are guiding disciples of Christ in the way they should go. This subject is of intense interest to everyone who is serious in trying to follow Christ.

Most people know that their lives can get horribly out of whack if they don't address the money question. Most people are recovering from some financial hardship . . . or afraid of one just around the corner. People truly need and, for the most part, will be interested to know biblical wisdom on money, stewardship, and generosity. To not preach on generosity in concrete and confident ways is to deprive those you serve of the most central teachings of Jesus.

But leave the brimstone at home; your intention in preaching isn't to shame or pile on guilt. Your mission in preaching generosity remains the same as any healthy approach to pastoral teaching: making plain God's Word to God's people. Perhaps you could select some of Jesus' parables that center on giving and build a series around that. Maybe you and your parish could walk alongside Paul's missionary journeys in Acts, understanding how generosity formed the early church. I would suggest spending three to four weeks developing the many incredible lessons that Paul gave us in 2 Corinthians 8–9. Go back even farther and look at the heart of the Old Testament prophets. Preaching is a tremendous opportunity to set a vision for how to use what God has given us.

I would suggest that the preacher stay away from topical preaching on this subject. If we just mash together some proverbs, warnings, slogans, and sayings found in the Bible, we miss the human drama behind the verses. And be cautious about trying to find too many faux tie-ins and links between what you want to say for today and what Jesus had to say for the people listening to him. Let me relate an example from my many moments attending conferences and seminars.

I attended a conference on the subject of this book. One resource supplier had assembled a small group Bible study program and was making it available for free to the attendees. The subject of the study booklet was finding financial wisdom for modern times. There were loads of good ideas for the modern family to help with saving, curbing their spending, investing, safeguarding, and giving their resources. This particular publisher had, however, stretched to find Bible verses to back up each of their many good ideas. But they were straining in a few spots. For example, the rationale given for saving money was the good Samaritan. Pointing to the fact that the man in the parable had money to leave the innkeeper and stood behind his offer to pay for all future expenses, the authors stated their point: it is biblical to have a savings account. After all, Jesus told a parable about a man who had and who used a savings account, the good Samaritan!

That, of course, is not the point of the story, as any reader would know. It is a fictional story in a historic setting that Jesus told to make a point about compassion and mercy coming from an unlikely source. At the end of the parable, he did not say, "Go and save likewise," hoping people would run off to the bank to open up a savings account! He was advocating for mercy, not for money!

Honestly, there is no need for such stretching to teach and preach a biblical message about generosity. Every bit of sound advice about money, generosity, stewardship, and investments will be found within the context of so much of the Bible. We really don't have to look that hard for verses or stories that apply. If your intention is to lift up the biblical value of generosity, you will see references, examples, teaching, and illustrations everywhere.

It was a thirty-year running joke at my church that I would always take three weeks to preach on the subject of stewardship and generosity. Indeed, I announced it! I promoted it. I gave advance notice about it, just to run counter to the apologetic ways some preachers will approach this subject. As I have said, people are very interested in this topic.

Undoubtedly you have heard it said that 80 percent of what Jesus spoke about was stewardship. I don't really believe that, of course. Neither do you. At least we don't believe that he spent 80 percent of all his time talking about money. But it *is* true that a vast majority of his recorded sayings and stories were about money, possessions, choices, obedience, and trust. It is not everything he said; not even most of what he said. But it is most of what has been recorded!

But we should take notice that even when Jesus taught on other subjects—mercy, justice, or unity—his parables often involved money. Jesus understood that earning, saving, and spending are huge parts of life; to speak as if economic realities didn't exist would have made him seem out of touch or irrelevant.

Remember: the main point of this book is to show that the early church wanted to emphasize and underscore that generosity was a life's choice; being called to follow Jesus was not just an intellectual assent to a body of teaching or a philosophy. Rather, it was a call to follow him. Every choice we make comes in the wake of that decision.

3. Tell It Slant

I want to add one note to this point about preaching generosity. It is a tender topic, and some preachers have abused their right to speak; they have shorn the sheep instead of borne the burden of pastoral care. In other words, some people listening to a series of messages on generosity may have been burned before. The wise preacher will want to address this tension right away.

There are two great ways to defuse the challenge of an awkward subject. One, as mentioned earlier, is to name it. Call it for what it is; lean into it and be clear, and be committed to not mincing words or shaving the edge off your points. The other method is to add healthy doses of humor to how you make the points. Humor is the great equalizer in any human situation; it allows us to say more things clearly and plainly without a lot of defensive pushback.

Why is this? Because truth is sometimes best heard when it comes to us at an angle, through a side door. Often our minds erect barriers around our closely held beliefs and assumptions that make it difficult for a speaker or preacher to penetrate. This is why one of the most effective elements of rhetoric is a story, particularly a humorous story. A good story well told usually brings listeners into our hearing. They are listening. And when the story reaches its conclusion, the listener can't help but "get it." The truth is told, but it is carried into the mind of the hearer through a narrative. And sometimes, especially with humor, the truth doesn't stand at the front door and knock to announce its arrival. Rather, with humor, the truth sneaks around to the side door, the servant entrance, and slips right in.

Employing another metaphor, Emily Dickinson coined a vivid phrase in a short poem. She used the metaphor of telling the truth "slant":

Tell all the truth but tell it slant —
Success in Circuit lies;
Too bright for our infirm Delight
The Truth's superb surprise.
As Lightning to the Children eased
With explanation kind,
The Truth must dazzle gradually
Or every man be blind.

Notice the last two lines. "The Truth must dazzle gradually / Or every man be blind." This is the point about storytelling, especially as Jesus did it. His parables were slanted in this same regard. He told the whole truth and nothing but the truth, but many times he revealed the specific truth in the shape of a story, or a parable.

Consider, for example, what Jesus is saying to us here: "Do not lay up for yourselves treasures on earth, where moth and rust destroy and where thieves break in and steal, but lay up for yourselves treasures in heaven, where neither moth nor rust destroys and where thieves do not break in and steal. For where your treasure is, there your heart will be also" (Matthew 6:19–21).

This is not a joke, as we might call it today. Rather, it is a tightly structured illustration that reveals truths about giving, stewardship, possessions, and generosity—on a slant, so to speak. We discover things as we consider this metaphor that we would resist if they were simply told to us straight.

Here are a few different takeaways from this simple but profoundly deep illustration. There are unseen forces that will always devalue and degrade our possessions: forces of nature (moth), forces of time (rust), and forces of sin (thieves). These happen outside of our notice. We never see moths eat, rust destroy, or thieves steal. Instead, the only investment method that makes sense is to lay up treasures in heaven. Heaven is a place of the supernatural (above forces of nature), the eternal (beyond the forces of time and rust), and perfection (not subject to the sinful effect of thieves). Our investments in heaven are safe.

Then Jesus delivers a profound truth that will change a person's life. Jesus says that our hearts can be directed by what we treasure. We saw this in the comments earlier about the expulsive power of a new affection. In short, we might say, "Attention directs intention." Whatever we pay attention to, that is what our hearts will love.

Again, Jesus is not telling a joke, but his illustration functions like a joke. It tells us something that we know is true, but its truth sneaks in through a side door. You get the stewardship lesson immediately. What is true of this illustration is true of parables, stories, and even jokes: while the setup may be fictional, the truth is real. That's "telling it slant."

Humor will help us understand deep points of stewardship, even if it is packaged in a really cheesy stewardship joke. Consider this groaner:

A man died and went to heaven. At the Pearly Gates, he met Saint Peter, who led him down the golden streets. They walked by mansions and beautiful estates until at last they came to the end of the road, where they stopped in front of a little shack. "This is your reward," Saint Peter told him.

When the man asked Saint Peter why he'd gotten a simple hut when there were so many mansions where he would be more comfortable, Saint Peter replied, "I did the best I could with the money you sent us."

This is not a secret way of preaching a version of a prosperity gospel. No one would ever take this idea literally, but they should take it seriously. It points out what the Bible says is clearly true: you can lay up treasures for yourself in heaven.

May I add one more piece of advice that many might hesitate to tell a preacher, teacher, or public speaker? Learn to tell a joke. Jokes are as much an art form as poetry. They are highly structured pieces of logical thinking (or illogical reasoning) with a twist in the end. Timing is important and practice is essential. Yes, I am very serious: practice telling jokes. A groaner is still a great joke if it is told well. But there is nothing that can be learned from a joke if it is poorly told.

4. Testify!

Giving up can't be a top-down process that the leader sustains. There may need to be a nudge from the pulpit, but there must be a way for those who are engaged in giving to share their hearts. This can take the form of testimonials on a Sunday morning, and those can be powerful. The testimonial must be carefully thought through and practiced. Like a good joke told poorly, a great testimony or personal story about giving that is not carefully considered will take away the impact.

It would almost never be a good idea to have a person share a testimony or relate a story to the congregation that the pastor had not personally heard, vetted, and helped to refine. I have seen too many teachable moments ruined by one man with a story that is unscripted and unrehearsed and that runs off unimpeded to chase rabbits, only to fall into a briar patch.

That is why I have always insisted that those who are going to bring their story to the large room need to write it out. If they do not, then I will lead them through their story as I stand with them and interview them. I will hold the microphone and say something along these lines: "You mentioned that you felt real joy when you started to give more generously. We don't need to know what that amount was, but what made you do it and what did it mean to you?" Asking open-ended questions in a public interview must be practiced as well.

As great as this method is for getting a story out, I find that something even more personal can be powerful. For years I conducted an annual program in which I would ask a large group of people, both as couples and singly, to write out a personal testimony as a personal letter to someone in the congregation. Or perhaps, even more daring and powerful, I might ask those who are more experienced in generosity not only to write letters, but also host dinners, lead a small group discussion, or speak to one of their ministry teams or groups within the church. People will listen to a peer. Remember: this isn't about creating some sort of prosperity gospel incentive for people to give so they can get more. But it is modeling. It is acting like a Barnabas to a Paul, or a Paul to Timothy.

One question might emerge from this suggestion: How does the pastor know who has a story that is worth telling? The answer is simple: ask the members of the church to volunteer either themselves or someone else. Believe me: people who have seen generosity take root in their lives have a story. It will usually be a story of personal transformation, trust, growth, risk, reward, and thanksgiving. I would encourage all pastors to trust that the Lord already has people in your church who have learned on their own some of the amazing lessons of the generous life. They may need help telling the story or writing it out, but it will usually bring inspiration to many.

Another limitation in telling stories is that for many churches, all financial information is a closely guarded secret. It is private information known only to the treasurer and the bookkeeper, for example. The senior pastor, who has the spiritual responsibility for the care of souls, is kept in the dark about who gives and what is given.

In my view, knowledge of what people give should not be a secret to those who are leading the church. It is essential information, as crucial as attendance, or an inventory of talents, or experience. When the pastor is kept in the dark about this information, it means that he is hobbled in his ability to create a generous culture. He cannot do it; he would never know if it was happening. In addition, as long as the giving records are sealed from the leader, the church's freedom to talk about money is also constrained. How can the church openly discuss money? No one knows anything about money and the level of giving.

The reasons why the senior pastor is kept in the dark about financial giving are well-known. It usually has to do with a possible temptation to show favoritism to some, to pay attention to the larger donors and ignore those who cannot give generously. I'd strongly recommend that lay leaders and church boards think a bit more highly of their spiritual leaders. And what does it say about the treasurer! Does he or she have a greater ability to resist such worldly temptations as favoritism?

It might be true that the pastor would be tempted to show more attention to the wealthy and less to the average givers. But as a seasoned pastor myself, I can say with authority that this is the least of the challenges of ministry. Pastors have a lot more reasons than money to look down on or unfairly admire members of a church. We have had to counsel people in the aftermath of their own terrible choices. Being light in the offering plate is nothing. Giving big doesn't make a big splash in light of everything else that can and does go awry. Pastors know that we are called to love and guide all people (and we do) in spite of the sins we have seen wreak havoc on their lives. If we can be trusted with *that* knowledge, I think we can be trusted with a little knowledge of what people give.

This is a controversial topic, to be sure. But this conversation is one worth having. I favor a philosophy that would bring the pastor into the full knowledge of all financial information.

5. Consider the Giver

As I've said, this is a book about reigniting generosity in your church, not a foolproof way to increase your church's budget. Creating a culture of generosity is also about creating a giving portal to the community through the church. As we saw in the case of the Macedonian churches earlier, they were giving direct aid to people far away in Judea. They didn't know the ultimate recipients of the gifts, but what if they had? What if the church could have taken up the offering and placed it for use within the local community?

Asked another way, what if your church could receive funds from the members and then disburse them to the needs and ministries in the local community? Can you imagine the reputation and the notoriety that your church would have? Almost instantly, the reputation of such a church would be, "That church is making a difference."

Few churches can do this, for obvious reasons. The church itself has financial obligations and ministries that demand its resources. So, when you hear about a church that is doing it, it impresses you. And if it would impress you, think of the locals.

One such church I read about recently seems to validate this vision of giving. Here is what I know about them.

Waterfront Community Church in Schaumberg, Illinois, was established near the beginning of the Great Recession in 2008. Today, it does the unthinkable: it gives away 100 percent of its weekly offering to charity. A few volunteer sponsors cover the administrative and fixed costs of the congregation so that the members can give away everything they collect during worship services. "My dream is every time a person puts a dollar in the plate, something happens," said the pastor, Rev. Jim Semradek. "When you give, you see a face on the other side that you're blessing."[2]

In connecting his parishioners' generosity directly to the people they are serving, Pastor Semradek has helped his congregation take a giant step toward restoring the body of Christ in his community to the esteem and admiration it once enjoyed throughout the known world. What this may tell us is that, instead of just lecturing people about giving, we ought to let them see the needs that they can help to fill. It may be that thousands of Christians in America are really hungry for the joy that comes with helping another human being in the name of Christ; we may just need to help them realize their hunger and show them how to satisfy it.

This is one of the common characteristics of newer, younger generations. They place support above subsidy, so to speak. They want to be involved in the work they give to. My generation (Boomers) has much more trust and confidence

---

[2] Manya Brachear, "Christians Want Say Where Money Goes," *Chicago Tribune*, November 18, 2008, http://newsblogs.chicagotribune.com/religion_theseeker /2008/11/christians-want.html.

in the institutions we have inherited from our parents (the Greatest Generation) or ministries we have built ourselves. We believe in the very modern understanding that people can be "deputized" or "appointed" to represent the interests and ministries of the larger culture. We (Boomers) believe in "representative government," as it were. But the millennial generation thinks very differently. They believe in "participatory government."

I should take this opportunity to say something else about the fascinating challenge of helping certain age groups accept and develop habits of generosity. Please consult the following list to see how or if your church is assisting different age groups to give for the work of the Lord.

- The millennials (born after 1981) came of age in an online world. In 2015, this age cohort became the largest living generation in the history of the United States.[3] They may not have available resources right now; many of them struggle with college debt, underemployment, and bad spending habits. But just wait. Things are going to change. Along with their slightly younger counterparts, this cohort is set to inherit over $40 trillion dollars (not a misprint: TRILLION) in the near future.[4] However, if you

[3] Richard Fry, "Millennials Overtake Baby Boomers as America's Largest Generation," Pew Research Center, April 25, 2016, http://www.pewresearch.org/fact-tank/2016/04/25/millennials-overtake-baby-boomers/.

[4] 21/64 and the Dorothy A. Johnson Center for Philanthropy, "#NextGenDonors," © 2013, http://www.acbp.net/pdf/pdfs-research-and-publications/nextgendonors-report.pdf, p. 4.

pass an offering plate down their pew, they might snap a picture of it and post it on Instagram (#Brass-Bowl), but they will not (generally speaking) put much of anything in it. They give like they read, chat, pray, date, flirt, and play: online. How do you reach them? INVOLVE THEM.

- Generation X (born 1965–1980) represents about 20 percent of the total giving population that live in the United States. These people are more established and can give larger amounts to the churches and causes they believe in. But the distinguishing mark of this group is that they want results. They want "bang" for every buck they donate. They want facts and transparent accounting. Where will my money go, and what will it do for the cause I am supporting? How do you reach them? INFORM THEM.

- Boomers (born 1946–1964) are the most awesome generation ever. (Just kidding.) They punch above their weight in donations by giving about 43 percent of all dollars given while making up only a third of the population. They love letters and they love to make month-by-month commitments. They will indeed sign a pledge card; their youngers will probably not. How do you reach them? INSPIRE THEM.

- The Olders (born before 1946) are the group that needs some help in learning how to give online or respond to an Internet appeal. They write and mail checks. They send thank-you notes. They may not crave involvement or activity in your church, but do not let that fool you. Sadly, many of them are living out their lives in isolation. They love company, but they often feel that life has moved on. They have made their mark on the world, and now some just want to make a difference . . . somewhere. Most of them check their e-mail about once a day. But they would love a personalized visit, letter, or appeal. How do you reach them? INCLUDE THEM.

6. Sing about the Heroes

Heroes define and encode our most important aspirations. If you want to really understand what motivates a community, a culture, a nation—or a church—you should get to know its heroes. In the last few years, I have been working on a national ministry project called Matthew 25. An anonymous donor kicked off the work, but by God's grace it will soon have a life of its own.

Matthew 25 is a kick-starter fund that is being made available to dozens and dozens of churches in the new Anglican Church in North America, of which I am a part. The concept is simple and wonderful. Money is set aside in a larger pool of funds. If a church or a nonprofit ministry wants to take on a new outreach or social justice program, they would apply for those funds. If awarded, the recipient of the grant must first raise its own funds to match the grant they have been awarded.

I was set in charge of the project two years ago. I set up the system, the pipeline of applications, the jury to decide, and the communication to the church fellowship. But the real hero is the anonymous donor who has given and pledged nearly $2 million to the program. His giving inspired the churches to dream about how they can enter their community to minister to the poor and needy. To me, the donor is a hero. He is anonymous, yes. But he has helped hundreds and hundreds of people through his acts of generosity.

Who are the other heroes of the church today? If you had to choose a person or group to illustrate your ideal, who would they be?

I might nominate someone like Greg and Alison Baumer, a young couple I heard about who live in Nashville, Tennessee. When his startup company was bought out, Greg received some $450,000—six weeks after starting his work! After Greg discussed the matter with Alison and with the other young men in his accountability group, he and Alison—with two children under school age and a six-figure student loan balance—made the joyful decision to give away 20 percent of their windfall.

Or maybe I would put forward Graham and April Smith, a young professional couple in New York City. Graham, a private investment banker, made a commitment a number of years ago to "reverse tithe": he lives on 10 percent of what he earns and gives away 90 percent. April, who works in a large investment firm, says, "Our idea is that an increase of income doesn't change your way of living; it changes your way of giving."[5]

---

[5] Generous Giving, "Graham and April Smith: Young, Urban, and Intentional" [online video], https://vimeo.com/143143025. accessed May 17, 2017.

I could keep going! I could talk about Rev. Herbert Bailey, with Church Army USA, who directs Uncommon Grounds Ministry in Aliquippa, Pennsylvania, a former steel town fallen on hard economic times. At Uncommon Grounds, Herbert and other volunteers offer sanctuary and fellowship to people as they seek to move them, in Bailey's words, "from isolation to community." Coordinating support from the Anglican Church North America's Matthew 25 Ministries as well as from about fifty churches, Uncommon Grounds provides a warm meal and a listening ear to those who come in. Often this leads to hope and a fresh start for those who have run out of other options.

I could talk about Nancy Cain McComb, a deacon and parish administrator in the Pittsburgh area, who felt God's urging to do something to help low-income, single moms. When she learned that an item essential to anyone caring for babies—diapers—was not covered by any of the federal low-income assistance programs, she realized that something as simple as providing diapers could take a huge burden off women who struggle from day to day to care for their children and themselves.

Through McComb's efforts, her parish has been galvanized to offer the time, energy, and generosity of Christians from ages five to ninety-five to purchase, organize, inventory, and provide for free the diapers that these hardworking single moms need so desperately. When these women come into the parish "diaper pantry" and find smiling, caring, giving Christians who are ready to help them at their point of need, they see the active love of Christ in an unforgettable way.[6]

I could easily extol the work of Chris and Carol Hermann, who are planting a church in a nursing home. That's right: a nursing home near Dayton, Ohio. Over the past two decades, they have been volunteering their time to organize other volunteers to give time to minister to this aging population. The residents of the nursing home they work with are particularly needy. They are low-income pensioners who have few if any relatives who stop by. The church becomes their family.

I spoke with this couple, and they described their church to me. Honestly, I didn't give it much of a second thought. But then these two ministers of the gospel told me offhandedly one day that about half of the new members come to faith in Christ sometime before they die. I was floored when I heard that statistic. Fifty percent. That is an unheard-of number in church ministry circles. I don't know what the number might be in reality, but the typical church has a heavy lift when it comes to bringing people to faith; especially the younger they are. But this nursing home is bringing one-half of their population to know and love the Lord before they die.

Isn't that really the point, anyway?

In every case, these are demonstrations of people who have caught the generosity bug. Though these humble servants

---

[6] "M25 Grant Recipients—Uncommon Grounds and Diaper Pantry," YouTube video, 4:22, an introduction to the Matthew 25 Initiative, posted by the Matthew 25 website, April 18, 2017, https://www.youtube.com /watch?list=PLMHcrUZEmlgWu54-g2Pxp6raSGgJgjl6m&v=SU7RoX2jHis.

would, of course, defer any praise or admiration to Christ, they are living the type of generosity-driven lives that bring honor to God and renewed respect to his church. They are pursuing lives of deep significance and joy, the type of lives that are worthy of imitation, as Paul suggested in 1 Corinthians 11 and elsewhere. By locating and celebrating heroes like these, we can set the church on a course to have a powerful, positive kingdom impact.

7. Go for the Ordinary

Building a culture of generosity means that the emphasis in the church month by month is consistent and clear. Focusing on the virtue and value of generosity is not phenomenal; that is, it is not extraordinary, but ordinary. The virtue should not be special; it is routine. It is not highlighted in one season and ignored after that; it is foundational.

As people begin hearing, then seeing, then experiencing for themselves the joys of giving up, there will be a temptation to nurture the high emotions and revival sentiment. As anyone who's ever been to summer youth camp can attest, though, living off a high spiritual moment isn't sustainable. Remind everyone that this is a daily adventure, and as Martin Luther King Jr. said, "If you can't fly, then run; if you can't run, then walk; if you can't walk, then crawl; but whatever you do, you have to keep moving forward."[7] Your goal is to shepherd disciples forward in this journey—some days they'll fly and some days they'll crawl.

---

[7] "Keep Moving from This Mountain," address at Spelman College on April 10, 1960, online at http://okra.stanford.edu/transcription/document_images /Vol05Scans/10Apr1960_KeepMovingfromThisMountain,Addressat SpelmanCollege.pdf.

That said, the year-round Christian liturgical calendar can create seasons of emphasis and experience that give a bit more oxygen to the virtue of generosity. For example, the season of Lent might be seen as a time not only for the internal reflection that is often imagined.[8] What if, instead, the entire congregation was asked to actually provide alms for some needy charity work in the name of Christ? Could a group of students be encouraged to give money toward Starbucks cards for every single staff person and teacher in their school as a gesture of love and thanks? Instead of scowling at the panhandling person who confronts us on the way to work, what if members were asked to give coupons to a restaurant instead? As a child growing up in the Episcopal Church, I fondly remember the mite boxes that were distributed to our Sunday school classes. They were filled with coins and bills for the forty days of Lent and given up as an offering. Over six decades later, I still remember the cardboard boxes and the place of prominence it had on my dresser at home.

The church season of Advent provides even greater opportunities for the encouragement and practice of generosity. A few years ago, Christmas morning fell on a Sunday. A church I am familiar with organized a massive, family-friendly outreach project. They did not have the foresight to take reservations or sign-ups for this event. And contrary to their best efforts to guess, the event was overrun with families and children eager to give. Hundreds of families showed up on Christmas morning, and it was a tremendous teaching moment

---

[8] For more on Lent, I recommend Aaron Damiani's great book on the subject, *The Good of Giving Up: Discovering the Freedom of Lent* (Chicago: Moody, 2017).

for the children. Indeed, it was an enormous "zag" on the typical family gift-fest that made a lasting impression on many.

There are other ways to develop a year-round emphasis on generosity, year by year. One of the best ways is this: replace every announcement in the service program with a snippet, sound bite, or pithy saying about generosity in the church. Brag on the people for practicing the joy of giving. Show pictures of ministry as it is happening every week. One pastor developed a great idea. He hired a young film student at the local college to make a short documentary called *A Day in the Life of St. Andrew's* showing the people and ministries of that congregation. It was broadcast on YouTube and included in parish-wide e-mail communication.

There are endless ideas and suggestions to share and to mention. But each parish and congregation will need to decide just how far this emphasis can go. As I mentioned in the introduction, we need the ecclesiastical equivalent of a Manhattan Project; an effort so big and so important that every aspect of congregational life is rethought and reimagined with generosity in mind.

8. Be Humble and Wise

A culture of generosity is not just about giving money "for the pews," as has been said. The church needs to lead and model the generosity it touts. Can the congregation itself be generous, and if yes, how?

There has been a good deal of study and thinking done about how the church can be generous. Models and methods from the past seem to fit easily into our expectations. We conceive of an outreach program and immediately we think of a soup kitchen or a Christmas gift giveaway. But we must be very wise and humble as we think about these avenues and programs. Sometimes our own need to participate unintentionally overpowers the dignity of the people we are trying to help. It truly is more blessed to give; most people reading this book would understand this. But givers must always consider the corollary: it may not be quite as easy to receive. For some, it can be embarrassing or humiliating. It can even be disempowering. Again, this is understandable. And the modern, giving church will be very sensitive to the recipients at this level.

For example, two important books in the last decade have called the church to reconsider its charitable outreach ministries. *Toxic Charity*, by Robert D. Lupton (New York: Harper-One, 2012); and *When Helping Hurts*, by Steve Corbett and Brian Fikkert (Chicago: Moody, 2014) have a common caveat in mind when it comes to Christians' eagerness to do good. "Not so fast," they say. Helping and ministry should empower the one being helped. The person being helped should always retain his or her human dignity and, in some way, participate in the effort to help. People in need should be enabled to stand for themselves and not just knocked flat with the love of others.

Christ Church's outreach ministry took this concern to heart as we began partnering with local initiatives. One of the first things we developed with many of the outreach ministries and service agencies in our community was a solid relationship with each board of directors. In fact, we developed a policy that put a church member on a board before we put that specific outreach ministry in our budget. We were not trying to be snobby, just sensitive. Rather than ask the obvious question, "What can we do here?" we wanted to start with a prior question: "How can we help these leaders serve the people God brings to them?"

Some of the most thrilling moments in my thirty-one-year run as rector were when we received special offerings for local causes or concerns. On so many occasions our church stepped up into the dizzying heights of support for a wide variety of causes, both foreign and domestic. We gave to overseas mission, hurricane victims, firefighters' children, flood victims furniture funds, and other disaster recovery projects. We took up special offerings at least eight to ten times a year.

The response was always staggering to me. A typical scenario would go something like this. A tornado would touch down in Oklahoma and displace a group of families. The local Anglican church would mount an outreach effort to help victims. I would announce on Sunday morning that we were taking up an offering all week long and would be sending it with an "away team" to the disaster zone the following weekend. Thousands of dollars would be given.

One weekend, we hosted the vicar of Baghdad, the Reverend Canon Andrew White. I took him to a special dinner party, a Saturday evening church service, and a full complement of Sunday morning services at Christ Church. At the end of the weekend, over $200,000 had been collected for his refugee and resettlement ministry. A year later I met the vicar in Jerusalem for dinner. He was still floating from his time in Plano. He freely admitted that the weekend in Dallas was a record. He had received the largest offering ever from any group of people in any part of the world. He added wryly, "Including the Pentecostals!"

9. Dream Big

We should also trust that God the Holy Spirit will move in the hearts and imaginations of our laypeople; he can be trusted to call and to act. When we become too institutional and set in our thinking, we can begin to push everything into a logical process. But as Einstein allegedly reminds us, "While logic will take you from A to B, imagination will take you everywhere." We sometimes need to be open to those with a wild idea.

Such was the case in an earlier period in the life of Christ Church. As I wrote the amazing story you are about to read, I sat on a plane, traveling back from a church conference. Writing this and remembering these tremendous events from earlier days of my leadership at Christ Church flooded me with joy, grief, thankfulness, and praise to God. I know I drew some strange looks from my seatmates too.

The story began when one of our staff members had an idea. Susan had been in the corporate world of J. C. Penney for many years. She began volunteering at Christ Church. Then, as we had an opening in the area of mission and outreach, she took the plunge and came onto our staff as a full-time leader. She was a tireless and focused worker for the Lord and had begun to build out the program and ministry, missions, and local community outreach. As she was retooling her own skills from the corporate world of smart business suits and net-net bottom lines, she was reading books about churches that galvanize around stepping out in faith, trusting that the Lord will bless, compound, and multiply their ministry. She began to wonder: *What would happen if . . . ?* And that led to a creative and exciting first step.

After a mission trip to an orphanage in Peru, Susan started reading a book that gave her an idea about raising money for the orphanage. In the book, a pastor gave $100 to each of his parishioners and challenged them to use this as seed money: to sow it and expect a bountiful harvest. Susan began to think about ten members of a team she led; what might they do with $100 each in "seed money"? Her only challenge was getting the funds that she needed: $1,000. But the very next Sunday, a check for $1,000 appeared in the collection plate, designated for missions. Susan had not mentioned her need to anyone but was now convinced that the Lord wanted us to go forward with the challenge.

She came to me, and I gave her permission to proceed. She called her Roof Dog Mission Team together and gave them each a copy of the book and a crisp $100 bill as a bookmark, along with the challenge to grow the money for the children in Peru. The results were of biblical proportion.

The ten team members were profoundly moved to accept the challenge. Ed, for example, used the funds to advertise an

"Upscale Treasure Sale" that became a church-wide event. It was so successful that it took over one of the buildings of the church for three days. This effort continued for three years and raised nearly $20,000.

Kym, a runner, decided to use the money to enter herself in a local 5K and then gain a few sponsors. That first year she raised hundreds of dollars. But the following year, she teamed up with a few others and sponsored a race for the community at the church—and their dogs. Thousands of dollars were raised for the orphanage. Year after year, the "Roof Dog Run" grew and grew and grew. Local businesses were tapped to give; a "Gold Sponsorship" went for $50,000. Runners and their dogs were invited, and they came. Our children's ministry planned special events for the youngsters. Police officers gave of their own time to provide support for the run. And year after year, tens of thousands of dollars were raised. That original $100 investment generated $250,000, given in the name of Christ to an orphanage in Peru—enough to build an entire new facility.

Other results from the $1,000 were, of course, less spectacular. One man even lost his book with its $100 bookmark in the backseat pocket of an airplane! Perhaps nothing came of it . . . or perhaps something even greater! But from Susan's $1,000 came hundreds of thousands of dollars—perhaps close to a million, all things considered. Not even Amazon, Apple, or Google can boast such a return on investment.

Generosity became the watchword for the church in those salad days of our second decade. This ministry alone blessed thousands, and through it, hundreds of members were empowered to serve. Members began to employ the simple ideas of "investment" and "seed" to their own giving. And while the financial giving for outreach swelled in the church, giving to the operational budget of the church never suffered.

More than that, public awareness of Christ Church increased. We became known as "the church that gives; the church that is making a difference." I know this because of the things that many leaders in the community told me. I cannot say, however, that the church grew in strength among the "leadership class" in the local community; it really did not. Very few of the political elite came to Christ Church. But our members who were fully involved and fully engaged in the outreach ministries of our church were ever more committed and were eager to invite their friends. In other words, we grew from the rank and file, not through the "leadership" class. As I read the letters of Paul to the Corinthians, I note this same phenomenon. The church did not grow among the elite, but among the everyday members of the community.

10. Build the Infrastructure

What Matthew 25 Ministries (number 6 in this chapter) and other such groups are doing is helping the church put in place the needed infrastructure for placing generosity back at the center of our message to the world. When we find heroes of generosity like those celebrated throughout the chapter, we need to be able to provide them a platform to facilitate, not only their giving, but the replication of such giving in the lives of other Christians.

One way the church can do this is by establishing, maintaining, and publicizing legacy funds: arrangements where generous givers can pool their resources and leverage them for greater impact. Matthew 25, for example, has received a generous matching gift from an anonymous donor who wishes to multiply the impact of the gift through churches and ministries all over the nation.[9] Can you begin to imagine the impact that $2 million could have when applied to ground-level efforts like those of Herbert Bailey, Nancy McComb, and others, as they meet the needs of hurting people in their communities, graciously serving them in the spirit of Christ? Or consider the impact of the generous Christians who underwrite the administrative and operating costs at Waterfront Community Church in Illinois, thus freeing church members to direct 100 percent of their weekly contributions, not to paying rent or ministers' salaries, but to directly addressing the human necessities of the people who live around them? In these ways, legacy funds like these become, rather than a monument to any single benefactor, a living, breathing source of abundant life, not only for those who receive the help, but also for those who provide it.

But we can think bigger than this. Remember what was said earlier: nearly $40 trillion changes generations in the next few decades. Shouldn't the transfer of wealth include a provision for the continued proclamation of the gospel? Churches should be active now helping individuals develop endowments and trusts for the missionary work of the Lord.

---

[9] M25, "About Us," https://matthew25i.org/about-us/, accessed May 20, 2017.

In other words, one way a church can be generous in the world of tomorrow is through the generosity of those who will name the church in their wills as a beneficiary.

This should not be a taboo topic of conversation within the church. In fact, it is a forgotten and often ignored obligation for every minister to have a conversation with members of the church about establishing a will. Yes, it is true. In the 1979 Book of Common Prayer the "Minister of the Congregation" is directed "to instruct the people from time to time about the duty of Christian parents to make prudent provision for the well-being of their families." Fair enough. That is a good thing. But the rubric goes on to include instructing the congregation "of the duty of all persons to make wills, while they are in health, arranging for the disposal of their temporal goods." Okay, but that is a far cry from asking that the ministry of the gospel be included as part of a personal last wishes. But read on. The statement goes on to strongly advise that the person leave bequests for religious and charitable purposes.

Here is the text in its entirety: "The Minister of the Congregation is directed to instruct the people, from time to time, about the duty of Christian parents to make prudent provision for the well-being of their families, and of all persons to make wills, while they are in health, arranging for the disposal of their temporal goods, not neglecting, if they are able, to leave bequests for religious and charitable uses" (Book of Common Prayer, 1979).

Don't tear the practical concern from the pastoral concern here. The great writer and thinker Leo Tolstoy was driven to the brink of suicide by this pivotal question: "Is there any meaning in my life that the inevitable death awaiting me does not destroy?" Is it not the pastor's role to help walk Christians through the most practical of answers to that question?

It seems to me that this should be on the top ten goals for every parish leader or rector. Remember what Paul said to Timothy: "Godliness with contentment is great gain, for we brought nothing into the world, and we cannot take anything out of the world" (1 Timothy 6:6–7). This sobering knowledge should fill the hearts of all generous believers with the determination to make Christian ministry go forward in strength by including gospel work in their wills.

Another vital piece of infrastructure for generosity involves complete transparency on the part of those administering the gifts. When we tell God's people the good news of what the body of Christ is doing for those in need, and when we openly share every detail of how the generous gifts of Christians are being received and distributed, we open the floodgates for even greater generosity. This, of course, assumes that we are truly acting as "faithful stewards of God's grace," as Peter instructed his readers in 1 Peter 4:10 (NIV). We who have received so much from God ought to gratefully funnel that blessing on to others. We should do it in such a way that, rather than questioning our motives or our openness, the world marvels at our unselfish sharing of the resources God is providing. When we do that, we unlock even more grateful hearts to participate with God in caring for his people.

These are some of the big ideas that have the broadest appeal, but the truth is that this list could just keep on going (and going and going). We could talk about even more tactical ideas: communication, asking members to donate appreciated stock, or setting up the most effective online and mobile giving portals. As you and your church become more invested in creating a culture of giving up, consider yourself invited to join an ongoing conversation. My blog (www.Leaderworks.org) will continue to post these more specific strategies as well as highlight new ideas from churches in all sorts of different contexts.

For now, it's my prayer that these ideas have ignited an imagination for your church's first steps toward giving up.

Also, please note the appendix in the back of the book. I have listed a dozen unique ideas, one of which might be the perfect next step for your church. And remember: send me your best ideas so they can be shared as well.

KEY POINTS

- Giving up is about forming a renewed culture of generosity in your church, not increasing budgets or extending programs.

- Establishing this culture involves all aspects of the church—from preaching to leadership training to lay testimonies to community involvement.

 DISCUSSION QUESTIONS

1. Run a quick diagnosis of your church's focus on generosity. Have you seen some of these values in action?

2. Do you disagree with any of these big ideas? What from your experience makes you feel this way?

3. Which of these seem most relevant for your church community to consider as you look to create a generous church?

CONCLUSION

In the early days of our parish, the North Dallas region was going through a recession. Businesses were struggling, and many people were being laid off. There was a dip in many industries, and people in the church were greatly affected. In December of that year, one of my parishioners stopped by the church to talk about a few things, and in the course of our conversation, he told me that his company had hit a wall. He was looking at red numbers for a long, long time. He was afraid. He was worried.

I tried to encourage him as best I could. When he asked for some financial advice, I knew I was in over my head. The only thing I remember saying to him was a very simple suggestion: "Why not make God your partner, and give up to him as he gives over to you?" That is all I can honestly remember saying. But my friend not only remembered it, but also made it his life's motto.

From that point forward, his life, his finances, his business, and his purpose were all about giving up. He celebrated it every fall for the next twenty years. By early October I would get a phone call from him and a request for some time to sit and talk. We'd talk about our families, politics, faith, business, church life, and such. Then, toward the end of our time, he would always fish inside his shirt pocket and draw out a folded check. He'd ask for a pen (I soon figured out that I should always have a pen with me!), and then he'd write out the check to the church for some proportion of his income, usually 10 percent. He'd fold it in half and press it between two fingers. He would often feign hesitation by shaking his hand or twitching his wrist away. But it was all in good humor. He loved the drama of the moment and squeezed every bit he could from it.

Basically, I was a pastor to this man and to his family. I had prayed at the bedside of his dying mother. I had led his son to faith in Christ and discipled him for a few years. I led the marriage service for his son and his new bride. I baptized the grandchildren. I oversaw his wife's spiritual growth through a women's small group Bible study. And I took a field trip with him one day to an out-of-town property to offer a house blessing. These are the privileges of a pastor, and I was honored to do these things with him and with so many others. What a joy it is to serve God in this way.

I came to have high regard for my friend as a brother in Christ. And when it was time to step down as rector and senior pastor of our church, I told him face-to-face. And when it was time to welcome the new rector, I set the meeting up. And yes, the ritual continues.

He came to give. Every year. And his gift to the Lord was a "giving up" of himself, his life, and his labor. Years earlier he had made God his partner and was simply offering his tithe back to the Lord in this annual moment.

But then he was tested.

A few years ago, I received a text from him instead of a phone call. He admitted that the year had been terrible: taxes and insurance had eaten his profits, and there would be nothing from him in that calendar year. He offered to get together for coffee anyway, and of course, I accepted.

I was impressed with his candor. His company was on life support. He would have loved to sell it. He was tired of the routine regulations that impeded his work. He was ready to let it all go. As his pastor, I was worried about his faith. I had seen him have good year after good year and now worried he might be going through a crisis of confidence. Believe it or not, the following conversation took place between a pastor and a member of his church completely by text:

> Me: Sorry to hear about your business hardship. I'll miss the offering for sure. We really have needed you every year. But I'm more concerned about you.

> Him: Thanks. I wish it were different.

> Me: Yes, me too. I hope you will continue to hope and trust God for what is to come.

> Him: If you are thinking that somehow I am having doubts about things . . . don't. I have complete confidence in God. I am so thankful for everything God has done for me. Giving has been a joy to me.

Me: Glad to hear that. God has been good . . .

Him: Yeah . . . I have seen him return it, over and over again in more ways than money. If one year or two he doesn't return it in that way, I can deal with that. He has given me too much to ever be a complainer.

Me: You need to preach this Sunday, and preach that message.

Him: I could do it in a shorter time than you do, for sure.

Then there was a long period of time between the next set of texts. The telltale sign of someone texting on the other end appeared on my screen . . . then it disappeared. What was this man thinking about now? What would he come back with? And when could we meet for coffee? I truly hate having this level of conversation by text. Minutes ticked by. I changed channels to see what was on. Wait a minute. He was probably watching the . . . yes, there it was: the Dallas Cowboys game. I knew it would be a while before I got a text back.

A few minutes after they blew the whistle at halftime, I heard my phone beep. Another text had arrived.

> Him: It all started when you told me to make God my partner. I've tried to do it, and if he chooses to let the business go broke, I'm good with that too. He's part owner!

> Me: That's awesome. I'll text you Monday for some coffee this week. I'm buying!

> Me: Great game by the way!!

What impressed me about this man was his openness to all the circumstances of life under the leadership of God. He was ready, eager, and willing to follow the Lord wherever he was led. This man had become a disciple who knew firsthand about giving up. He gave and gave and gave as the Lord had given to him. It is easier, one might think, to give as the Lord has given to you as long as the Lord gives first! But that was not his heart. In fact, it was giving that had changed his heart. And when there was nothing to give one year . . . he gave his faith and his hope and his confidence in the Lord instead.

This is the hope and the promise of joyful obedience to the Lord in the matter of generosity. As Paul would attest of the Macedonians, so I have seen in my years of ministry: there is great joy in giving. I have seen it in the lives of thousands of people. I have known it in the life of the Christ Church community. I have felt it personally in my own family. I have seen it played out in great ways in the lives of our adult married children. They continue to give generously to their own churches.

If every pastor's prayer is that "Christ is formed" (Galatians 4:19) in the hearts and lives of the people, then many of my prayers have been answered. Remembering the opening story about the Latin motto that vexed me, I saw that it could apply to Christian men and women who embraced the call to generosity. *Esse Quam Videri.* Generous givers don't just "seem to be" people who love and serve the Lord. They are real. They are changed by their giving. And under God, these changed lives are a tribute to the effectiveness of the gospel and a living testimony to an unbelieving world. Giving is the new evangelism; it proves the gospel is real. Giving is the new discipleship; it puts the gospel into motion. As we give up to the Lord, we become more and more like him as he gave up his own life to God. As we practice the way of giving our lives up, we also become more and more like the One who gave up his life for us!

A Dozen More Tips for Instilling Generosity

The key to creating a culture of generosity starts with focus. And as I've argued, putting your church's focus on giving doesn't force you to sacrifice the church's mission. In the New Testament and throughout the history of the church, evangelism has been most effective when the church was famous for giving. We've also seen that Christian formation only affects the heart when disciples are called to do more than sit and learn; instead, we have to follow our Master in his work.

How you help bring that focus to your church is going to vary depending on your context. There are countless ways of instilling a virtue of generosity, and I have no intention of indexing them all here. But I did want to provide some tactical, granular ideas from my long experience in ministry. The following list is only a brief overview of what could be possible or appropriate in your context. As readers and leaders reflect on this list, new ideas and other creative ways of encouragement and education will surely emerge. As ideas are submitted through the website, they will be vetted and posted on a growing list. Check back with www.leaderworks.org for updates.

Pray for the People

This is an obvious step, of course, but it's important to remember that ministers don't pray for the spiritual lives of their parishioners and *then* pray that giving might increase. Those aren't two separate categories. We pray that the members of our church would have their hearts softened enough to begin giving generously, and we pray against the sins that might be keeping members from giving. And we rejoice to see the work God is doing in the lives of those who have begun to give up. Every minister must carry the burden to pray for all aspects of our members' lives, and that most certainly includes praying for generosity in their financial lives. Also consider including specific prayers for giving in the weekly worship.

Offer Prayers for Employment

Work creates the currency that we use to live our lives. We must have work to earn money to pay for the things we need, want, and give. Those who are unemployed are in need of the prayers of the church. Could the church offer to pray for those men and women who are looking for a job? What would be the effect on a congregation if the minister asked all unemployed people who are looking for jobs to stand up and allow the church body to pray for them?

For able-bodied workers, being "let go" or laid off or "right-sized" out of a job is one of the most humbling moments in their lives. As pastors, we cannot treat this lightly. But we cannot ignore the plight of many in our churches who need to find work. Why not pray for them? Why not let the body of Christ know its own need?

I have been in our community for more than thirty years as pastor and rector of the same church. During that time we have undergone several recessions. I can remember many occasions when I would announce that in a week or so to come, I would offer special prayers for those who were unemployed. Attendance was normal that Sunday when I called for those who needed special prayer for work to come forward. Many came up . . . but I knew that many were embarrassed and remained hidden in their pews. Nevertheless, we prayed. And as we prayed, members and friends became aware that some of their fellow members and friends were in need. And frankly, unbeknownst to me, money and gift cards began to appear anonymously in the mailboxes of those who expressed their need.

Create New Means

Most people don't walk around with checkbooks anymore. If you have any doubt of this, ask anyone under thirty-five if he or she is carrying a checkbook. You will hear silence. Everything is done online or via the debit cards people carry in their purses and wallets. Ask any banker. Ask any usher in a church! Fewer and fewer checks are being written.

When someone desires to give on a Sunday morning for a special cause, he or she may not be able to meet that desire with an action. Your church may have already found a solution for online giving that works for you, but if you haven't,

I would recommend Kindrid.com. (There are other apps and websites too; the technology is amazing!) Apps and websites such as this one lower all barriers to giving, allowing easy text-to-give, online, and in-app giving.

It is probably best to pressure-test this kind of giving on a few special-event weekends or for a unique giving project (such as funding a missionary, perhaps) before it becomes a feature in your church. But in my consultation with the management of "Text to Give" companies who provide this service, I have learned that they are clearly optimistic about the future of their model. They see no diminishment of giving either. Their research shows that people give at or above the average gift even if by text.

As Jesus might have said, "The Spirit is willing, but the checks are weak."

Install a Lockbox

You'll be shocked to hear this, but sometimes—sometimes!—people put things off until the last possible minute. Some members intend to give but somehow end up desperate to donate in the last week of the year. I know, I know . . . it seems unlikely. But we installed a lockbox at Christ Church years ago, and it's been used every year on December 31 . . . by more people than I will ever tell.

Encourage Donation of Appreciated Stock

This is a little technical, but if you can communicate this to your members, you can provide them a way of giving most have never even thought of. When the markets are on the upswing, many people will find they have significant growth (officially, "unrealized capital gains") in many securities in their taxable (non-retirement) accounts. If they sell those securities to free up cash for their end-of-year giving, they will likely incur tax on those gains. (If the security was held longer than a year, the tax rate is usually 15 percent, but if it was short-term [less than a year], the gain will generally be treated as "ordinary income" and taxed at the person's marginal tax bracket—which could be as high as 39.6 percent.)

Instead of selling the security, a better idea may be to gift the security in-kind to the church (or any charity, for that matter). The donor, if he or she itemizes, gets to write off the total value of the security against ordinary income, and the church, which does not have to pay any tax on the sale, nets the full value of the security—a win-win for the church and the donor. We'll thank Uncle Sam for donating the difference!

Overcommunicate

Here is a grab bag of good ideas that some readers may find helpful:

- Since giving doesn't just happen by dropping checks in the offertory plate, make sure everyone knows how to give. Whether it's in the newsletter, the bulletin, or even a simple slide on a screen, it's crucial that members know their options and have easy access to giving. This is also a great use for your social media platforms.

- Remember that real transparency matters. It makes the needs of the church plain, and it connects the giver to the gift.

- Put a simple graphic into the bulletin every week, consisting of just two bars: Year-to-Date Giving and Year-to-Date Expenses. This is simple, clear, and—most important—objective. There's no obnoxious guilting about it, just the plain facts.[1]

- Write a year-end or special direct appeal letter annually. *Never write from a position of fear or to engender guilt for not having given.* GUILT CAN NEVER MOTIVATE. *Uphold and uplift; don't scold and demand.*

Develop Stakeholders

Focus key communication about generosity, needs, opportunities, and success on a small subset of the entire church. This might sound a bit controversial, if not elitist, so let me explain. Every church has a cadre of people who are deeply committed to its ministry. They are the volunteers, ministers, workers, and leaders of programs within the congregation.

---

[1] It might be tempting NOT to include a budget/expenses chart if the church is ahead of schedule. But I think that is a bit shortsighted. If the church has more money received than expended, celebrate that fact. Be open and honest in all reporting, even the good news! (If the church has consistently more money received than spent, then I'd advise that the budget be increased! Spend what the Lord enables.)

Larger donors would be included in this group. That list is a "leader list" and should be treated as the only subcategory for parish communication. After all, the vestry is a subcategory of communication. They receive "vestry-only" letters. Small group Bible study leaders are on their own mailing list as well. I am simply advocating for a new category for communication: stakeholders.

For example, if attendance at your church is three hundred, chances are there are about sixty people who will make up the core membership. This is the group who will carry the church forward in its ministry. They should be the focus of extreme attention and communication by the senior pastor and staff. As they grow and mature in their faith, their commitment and excitement will create a "halo effect" for the rest of the church. Their commitment and strength will extend and motivate others.

Some might object to this segmentation as exclusivist. It is not. Anyone can join the 20 percent—anyone. The invitation for greater involvement and commitment is always being offered, and new people are always being welcomed. And the very process of supporting stakeholders will naturally help bring new people in.

Leaders often make the mistake of focusing entirely on activating the uninvolved or the under-committed. It is usually a waste of energy and an exercise in frustration and anger. Instead, empower and inform the most committed; the already-involved. If they are being keyed into the mission of the church, they will bring many others in their wake.

Discover Needs

If a generous church is going to make inroads into the community around it, its leaders and members must understand who lives around the church. Oftentimes, new churches are so busy struggling to stay afloat that they focus on their own survival needs. This is understandable. Older churches are often out of touch with the changing demographics in their neighborhood. But again, a generous church is going to find ways of giving itself of the life of the community around it.

One very helpful resource is the Racial Dot Map offered on the website of the University of Virginia Weldon Cooper Center for Public Service. It shows a detailed map of the United States, based on the 2010 census. Each ethnic group is assigned a specific color, and every person in America is depicted by one dot. The details and the information are amazing, especially as one considers the massive immigration trends in the world and into the United States.

Check out this webpage and prepare to be amazed: http://demographics.coopercenter.org/racial-dot-map/.

Bless Outside Groups

There are dozens and dozens of ways that your church can encourage a culture of generosity. All it takes is a little imagination. Here are some examples:

- Each schoolteacher receives a gift on the first day of class: an envelope with a packet of instant Starbucks coffee in it. An enclosed friendly note might read: "We'd love to take you for coffee or tea, but we know you're busy teaching our children. Thank you and God bless you."

- Special offerings taken during the week of Thanksgiving (the two Sundays on either side of Thanksgiving and Thanksgiving Day) are designated for a local mission effort.

- Social media augments specific mission efforts or local ministries via the congregational platform. In other words, what if the church took on a special appeal for a local ministry and encouraged members to share it on their own social media channels? What if the church leadership offered to pay all service fees (usually about 2.5 percent) for a period of time for its members if they give through an online platform?

Recruit Food Trucks

One of the greatest and most creative ideas for generosity I have come across is from St. George's Church, Burlington, Ontario, Canada. During the summer months they open up their building and invite local food trucks to park in their parking lot to serve anyone who might come for a kind of "tailgate party" at the church. The church does the advertising and communication to its membership and the neighborhood. Hundreds of families attend every week for an evening of food, fun, and engagement with the church campus. The church, the playground, and most of the classrooms are all open to the public. Local business food trucks are blessed. And families have an inexpensive night out.

Give Small Group Assignments

If a church is going to get serious about developing generosity, it has to allow its members to practice generosity in other places besides the offering plate. This is a key understanding: increasing a culture of generosity is not all about having more money given to the church. It is about having more giving coming from its members and leaders. Could groups of people take on generosity assignments during the week and report back what they discovered? What happened to the server when a large tip was left? What did it feel like to give anonymously to a family in need or a young church?

Practice "Twice Is Nice"

Are there new church plants starting around you? Often they have little money to pay for the supplies and space they need. What would it be like to pass the offering plate twice on a Sunday: once for the home church and once for the new church plant?

Full disclosure: During my ministry at Christ Church, we started five churches. While the church was fairly generous in sending people, supplies, and salaries for staff, we were not generous in sustaining the new work. We considered those who left with the church plant to be a sustaining gift. We lost their giving to the mother church, and the daughter church gained their giving. But we could have done more, so we did. During the last two or three years of my leadership, we gave away 2 percent of our total revenue to church plants, near and far. Planters would attend our vestry meetings and share their vision for the church. Our vestry gave from our designated church planting funds.

LEADERWORKS

Please visit the **LeaderWorks** website for updated ideas and tools that others have found helpful.

If you have an idea, send it in.

Go to ***www.LeaderWorks.org*** for more information.

CPSIA information can be obtained
at www.ICGtesting.com
Printed in the USA
BVHW07s1735050918
526585BV00012B/537/P